The Decent Society

The Decent Society

Avishai Margalit

Translated by Naomi Goldblum

HARVARD UNIVERSITY PRESS
Cambridge, Massachusetts
London, England
1996

Copyright © 1996 by the President and Fellows of Harvard College
All rights reserved
Printed in the United States of America

Library of Congress Cataloging-in-Publication Data

Margalit, Avishai, 1939–
    The decent society / Avishai Margalit ; translated by Naomi
Goldblum.
        p. cm.
    Includes bibliographical references and index.
    ISBN 0-674-19436-5 (alk. paper)
    1. Civil society. 2. State, The. 3. Humiliation. 4. Justice. I. Title.
JC336.M35 1996
320'.01'1—dc20   95-42273

For Mira, Yotam, Tamar, and Ruth

Contents

Preface

Some twenty years ago I accompanied Sidney Morgenbesser to the airport. In the lounge, while waiting for his flight, we discussed Rawls's theory of justice, which had deeply impressed us both. Before parting, Morgenbesser announced to me—as well as to all the other passengers—that the urgent problem was not the just society but the decent society. To this day I am not sure what he meant by this, but the expression made a great impression on me. This book owes its existence to that remark of Morgenbesser's. I myself owe Morgenbesser much of my philosophical apprenticeship and not a few of my social persuasions.

The idea of the decent society appealed to me, but for many years I was not able to flesh it out. Gradually conversations I had with Palestinians during their uprising (the Intifada) in the occupied territories, as well as conversations I had with new immigrants to Israel from the countries of the defunct Communist bloc, convinced me of the centrality of honor and humiliation in the lives of people—and, consequently, of the importance that ought to be allotted to the concepts of honor and humiliation in political thought. Thus the idea was born of the decent society as a society which does not humiliate.

This book is not, however, about the Intifada or the downfall of Communism: these serve as illustrations only. Yet the book was written with the Israeli reader in mind, and it was written in Hebrew. It was David Hartman, among others, who convinced me that there might be a wider audience for the notion of the decent society than the Hebrew reading public. With his active encouragement and through the Shalom Hartman Institute in Jerusalem which he directs, a translation was sponsored. Naomi Goldblum bore the brunt of the task and carried it through with dedication.

Friends who read various drafts of the book helped me a great deal: Maya Bar-Hillel, Moshe Halbertal, David Heyd, Joseph Raz, and Michael Walzer. I want to thank them all. My wife, Edna Ullman-Margalit, my life partner and my work partner, helped me in the larger contours as well as in the smaller details. To thank her is not enough.

Institutions also helped. My stay as a Visiting Fellow at St. Antony's College, Oxford, provided me with a decent society for writing large chunks of this book. The pleasant library of the Van Leer Institute in Jerusalem, where I have been spending most of my waking hours for many years, made it possible for me to write more. Other support was provided by the Center for Rationality and Interactive Decisions of the Hebrew University of Jerusalem. The finishing touches were given to the book in the warm and wonderful home of my friends Irene and Alfred Brendel in Hampstead. All of them have my gratitude.

This is not a textbook. The length of the various chapters and sections reflects not their relative weight but, rather, what I felt I had to say about their topics. I believe every sentence of this book to be true. I also believe that there are sentences in this book which are erroneous. This state of affairs is referred to by philosophers as the Preface Paradox. Whatever the logical status of this paradox, it is clear to me that it well reflects my own state of affairs.

I have written this book out of conviction. Conviction does not make one immune to error; if anything, it enhances its likelihood. I do not doubt that this book contains errors. I only hope that it contains enough truth.

Jerusalem
August 1995

Last night the Sheik went all about the city, lamp in hand, crying, "I am weary of beast and devil, a human being is my desire."

Rūmi (1207–1273)

Introduction

What is a decent society? The answer I am suggesting is roughly the following: A decent society is one whose institutions do not humiliate people. I distinguish between a decent society and a civilized one. A civilized society is one whose members do not humiliate one another, while a decent society is one in which the institutions do not humiliate people. Thus, for example, one might think of Communist Czechoslovakia as a nondecent but civilized society, while it is possible to imagine without any contradiction a Czech Republic which would be more decent but less civilized.

Social institutions can be described in two ways: abstractly, by their rules or laws, or concretely, by their actual behavior. Analogously, one can speak of institutional humiliation by law, as manifested by the Nuremberg Laws or those of apartheid, in contrast to concrete acts of institutional humiliation, such as the Los Angeles police officers' treatment of the black motorist Rodney King. In the concrete description of institutions the distinction between a noncivilized and a nondecent society is blurred. My interest in institutions is focused on their concrete

aspect, and so this distinction may become blurred quite
often in this book. But even if it is not always clear how
the distinction applies in particular cases, it is nevertheless
a distinction with merit. The idea of a civilized society is
a microethical concept concerned with the relationships
between individuals, while the idea of a decent society is
a macroethical concept concerned with the setup of the
society as a whole.

The concept of a decent society may be compared and
contrasted with other evaluative terms—for example, that
of a proper society as one that adheres to due process, or
that of a respectable society as one that protects its citizens'
respectability. But the most important comparison is between a decent and a just society. Clarifying the concept
of a decent society requires not only elucidating the contrast between decent and nondecent societies but also
comparing it with other social notions, whether rival or
complementary. I do not explicitly compare the notion of
a decent society with alternative social notions aside from
that of a just society, but I mention the possibility of
comparison in the hope of illuminating it throughout the
book.

In Part I, I discuss the reasons for feeling humiliated.
I begin with two radical claims. One is that of anarchism:
the very existence of governing institutions is a reason for
feeling humiliated. The other is that of Stoicism: no governing institutions can provide reasons for feeling humiliated. Both of these extreme claims are rejected in favor
of the assertion that governing institutions do not necessarily humiliate people, but they are able to do so.

The concept of a decent society, I maintain, is not
necessarily connected with the concept of rights. Even a

society without a concept of rights can develop concepts of honor and humiliation appropriate for a decent society. The appropriate concept of honor is the idea of self-respect, as opposed to self-esteem or social honor.

Part II deals with the question of what justifies according human beings respect. Three types of justification are presented. The first is a positive sort, which relies on a common human trait due to which people deserve to be respected. The second is a skeptical justification, which casts doubt on the possibility that such a trait exists, and suggests the attitude of respect itself as the source of respect. The third is a negative justification, which claims that there is no positive or skeptical justification for according humans respect, but there is a justification for avoiding humiliating them.

In Part III, I discuss the idea of humiliation as the rejection of a person from the human commonwealth and as the loss of basic control. I show how these two aspects of humiliation are manifested concretely in social setups as the rejection of specific forms of life in which people express their humanity.

Part IV deals with the way major social institutions, such as those involved in welfare or punishment, must act in a decent society. I do not attempt to cover all social institutions (housing, for example, is not discussed), but a wide variety of institutions is surveyed.

The book is thus divided into two main sections. The first three parts deal with humiliation; the fourth part discusses its institutional manifestations. At the end of the book I compare the decent society with the just society. Every just society must be a decent one, but the opposite does not hold.

I have not set an upper or lower limit on the size of the social units that are candidates for decent societies, but in the modern world the natural choice is societies on the order of magnitude of a nation. Smaller social units will not quite do. One reason for this is that the conditions for nonhumiliating life today require at least the ability to read and write, as well as some basic technical skills, which in turn require a relatively advanced educational system. It is difficult to provide such an educational system in a small society. Nations are also of interest for another important reason. States are supposed to have a monopoly on the use of force, and they quite often actually do. Thus the state has an especially great potential, both normatively and factually, for institutional humiliation.

I began with a rough characterization of a decent society as a nonhumiliating one. Why characterize the decent society negatively, as nonhumiliating, rather than positively, as one that, for example, respects its members? There are three reasons for this: one moral, one logical, one cognitive. The moral reason stems from my conviction that there is a weighty asymmetry between eradicating evil and promoting good.[1] It is much more urgent to remove painful evils than to create enjoyable benefits. Humiliation is a painful evil, while respect is a benefit. Therefore eliminating humiliation should be given priority over paying respect.

The logical reason is based on the distinction between goals which can be achieved directly and intelligently and those which are essentially by-products and cannot be achieved directly.[2] People who want to be spontaneous, for example, cannot do so directly by deciding to. The most they can do is pretend to be acting spontaneously.

Spontaneity is essentially a by-product rather than a primary goal. According people respect may also be essentially a by-product of one's general behavior toward people, while this is not true of nonhumiliation. Perhaps there isn't any behavior that we can identify as extending respect (in the sense that there are specific acts that we identify as bestowing military honor, such as saluting). Perhaps we simply grant respect through acts intended for other purposes, so that the respect granted is only a by-product. In contrast, there are specific acts, such as spitting in someone's face, that are humiliating without being by-products of other acts.

The third, cognitive, reason is that it is easier to identify humiliating than respectful behavior, just as it is easier to identify illness than health. Health and honor are both concepts involving defense. We defend our honor and protect our health. Disease and humiliation are concepts involving attack. It is easier to identify attack situations than defense situations, since the former are based on a clear contrast between the attacker and the attacked, while the latter can exist even without an identifiable attacker.

All these are reasons for choosing to characterize the decent society negatively rather than positively. In a positive characterization, a decent society is one that accords respect through its institutions to the people under its authority. As we shall see, it will sometimes be necessary to use this positive characterization of the decent society as well as the negative one we began with.

I have tried not to classify the decent society under the familiar "ism"s of liberalism or socialism. If labels cannot be avoided, then the one that best fits my idea of a decent society is "Orwell's socialism," as opposed to Orwellian socialism. The latter is the animal farm of equal and more equal, rather than a human society of equal human beings. Orwell is certainly an important source of inspiration for the idea of the decent society, and in the sense that Orwell was a socialist, the decent society embodies Orwell's socialism.

I

The Concept of Humiliation

1

Humiliation

Humiliation is any sort of behavior or condition that constitutes a sound reason for a person to consider his or her self-respect injured.

This a normative rather than a psychological sense of humiliation. On the one hand, the normative sense does not entail that the person who has been provided with a sound reason for feeling humiliated actually feels that way. On the other hand, the psychological sense of humiliation does not entail that the person who feels humiliated has a sound reason for this feeling.

The emphasis is on *reasons* for feeling humiliation as a result of others' behavior. Feelings have not only causes but also reasons. There is a sound reason for feeling afraid of a free-roaming tiger. Under normal circumstances there is no sound reason for feeling afraid of a common housefly. Of course, not only behavior is liable to humiliate people. Conditions of life are also capable of providing sound reasons for feeling humiliated. Conditions are humiliating, however, only if they are the result of actions or omissions by human beings. Conditions ascribed to nature cannot be considered humiliating on my view. Richard III, who was so deformed that even dogs in his vicinity snarled at him, had an excellent reason for bemoaning his bitter fate, but he lacked a sound reason for feeling humiliated, as long as we ascribe his deformity to nature rather than to any action or omission by human beings. Only humans can produce humiliation, although they need not actually have any humiliating intent. There can be no humiliation without humans to bring it about, but there can be humiliation without humiliators, in the sense that the people causing the humiliation did not intend to do so.

There is a secondary, metaphorical, sense in which people see the very conditions of human existence, such as old age, handicaps, or ugliness, as reasons for feeling humiliated. The secondary or metaphorical sense of humiliation is not humiliation in my use of the term. This is because the secondary sense involves humiliation as a result of natural life conditions. The difference between my use of the term and that of people who use it in its secondary sense is not that I require the existence of a humiliator while they do not. The difference is in our view of nature. They do not consider nature a neutral agent; they consider it to be guided by God. Thus in their view there is someone who can use the conditions of nature to humiliate or exalt people. It is possible that what lies behind this view is a hidden assumption that God is the humiliator.

A decent society is one that fights conditions which constitute a justification for its dependents to consider themselves humiliated. A society is decent if its institutions do not act in ways that give the people under their authority sound reasons to consider themselves humiliated.

This proposed account of humiliation, and thus of the decent society, stands in need of much clarification and explication. It is worth beginning, however, by confronting this account with two diametrically opposed reactions that can serve as warning signals. The first is anarchism, which claims that any society founded on ruling institutions is by definition a humiliating society. This view maintains that any society with permanent institutions necessarily consists of rulers and ruled, and that to be ruled is a sound reason for feeling humiliated. At the opposite end of the spectrum is Stoicism, which claims that no society can be humiliating, because no society can provide a thinking person with good reasons for feeling humiliated. The reasoning behind this view is that humiliation is an injury to a person's self-respect, and self-respect is tautologically the respect persons accord themselves without needing the opinion of others. Self-respect is independent of any action or omission by other people toward one, whether one is a slave like Epictetus or an emperor like Marcus Aurelius.

There is another view that should be considered, which I call the Christian view. In essence it is the idea that the most deadly sin is pride, and that pride can only be cured by humility. People who are subject to a humiliating society undergo an edifying experience in the war against pride. A humiliating society is a formative experience for those who are trying to become humble. A humble person has no sound reasons for feeling humiliated. A humiliating society hurts those who ought to be humiliated, namely proud people, while people of higher morality, namely humble people, cannot be humiliated by others. Jesus' Via Dolorosa is a paradigm of experience with a continuous stream of humiliations:

> And they stripped him, and put on him a scarlet robe. And when they had plaited a crown of thorns, they put it upon his head, and a reed in his right hand; and they bowed the knee before him, and mocked him, saying, Hail, King of the Jews! And they spit upon him, and took the reed, and smote him on the head. And after that they had mocked him, they took the robe off from him, and put his own raiment on him, and led him away to crucify him. (Matthew 27:28–31)

Even if this temptation was not a good reason for Jesus to consider himself humiliated, those who put the crown of thorns on his head had a sound reason for considering themselves humiliators. The lesson Christians are supposed to learn from Jesus' humiliating journey is to consider humiliating behavior as a trial rather than a sound reason for feeling humiliated. The fact that there is no such reason, however, does not absolve the humiliator of the grave sin of pride and arrogance, since the humiliating acts are intended to prove one's superiority over the other.

Anarchism: No Governing Institutions Are Decent

Anarchists play the role in the political realm that skeptics play in the cognitive realm. Skeptics question the very existence of propositions that can be known—that is, beliefs that can be justified as knowledge in principle. They claim that no possible justification of a belief can turn it into knowledge. Analogously, anarchists are people who claim that no possible governing order based on force can be justified in principle. In science the skeptical claim is the so-called null hypothesis—namely, the claim that there is nothing to explain because the phenomenon that is supposed to be explained is merely a chance occurrence. Philosophical skeptics and anarchists each propose a "null hypothesis" in their own area: they claim there is nothing to justify. What seems to be a candidate for justification actually cannot be justified. If political philosophy attempts to answer the question, "What is the source of justification for political authority?," the anarchist retorts that there is no possible justification—political authority is a sad fact and not something that can be justified. The anarchist's null hypothesis is the following: no society with permanent (as opposed to ad hoc) institutions can be a decent society.

How can we understand the concept of humiliation underlying anarchist doubts about the possibility of a decent society? For the anarchist, humiliation means curbing the autonomy of individuals through coercive institutions. Governing institutions exercise their coercive power over the people subject to their authority by distorting the subjects' order of priorities. Distortion of the order of priorities through which people express their autonomy constitutes humiliation. Therefore coercion constitutes humiliation. The claim made by anarchists is actually even stronger: the very possibility of coercion—that is, the very fact that people are subject to the good graces of an authority—constitutes humiliation. In order for people under authority to be humiliated it is not necessary for the authority to actually be coercive—it is enough that it constitutes a permanent threat hanging over the people under the institution's authority.

I assume that even anarchists would agree that the referee in soccer, even though he has the authority to compel obedience—for example, to throw out a rowdy player—is not necessarily a humiliating institution. Anarchists would refuse, however, to see the institutions of a society which constitutes a state as similar to soccer referees. They do not accept the liberal idea of the state as a referee. Like Marxists, they believe that the state is an active player. Underlying this anarchist claim is the belief in a sort of "iron law of oligarchy," which states that whenever there are institutions there are always rulers and ruled.[1] Not only does each institution have its rulers and its ruled, but across the various institutions the rulers are the same rulers and the people ruled are more or less the same people too. Soccer—at least nonprofessional soccer—is not a typical case of a governing institution. Rather, it is a voluntary organization for a limited purpose, which can be (relatively) isolated from other ruling organizations. Ruling institutions—that is, those having the means to compel obedience—are actually oligarchies. And oligarchy means the systematic humiliation of people under the authority of permanent rulers.

The anarchist view I have presented here—which is not, as far as I know, a view advanced by any historical thinker—is based on problematic assumptions, some conceptual and some factual. One of the conceptual assumptions, for example, is that humiliation is any possible diminution of a person's autonomy. Another is that autonomy is expressed in a person's order of priorities, so that a distortion of this order constitutes humiliation. Among the factual assumptions might be included, for example, the assumption of the "iron law of oligarchy."

But in spite of the problems with the anarchist view, it is important to examine it because it presents the "null hypothesis" for our discussion. According to this view any attempt to portray a decent society in terms of nonhumiliating institutions is an enterprise with an inherent contradiction. Institutions are humiliating by their very nature. Dealing with the anarchists' "null hypothesis" is an issue for this book as a whole and not for a hasty answer here. I therefore confine myself to a few comments highlighting the challenge this view poses to our discussion.

At first glance it may seem easy to refute the anarchist view with the argument that the power of ideological anarchism is totally dependent on the proposal by political anarchists of an alternative society devoid of governing institutions—an alternative that does not exist. In the absence of an alternative, one may suspect that such a society would not be able to exist for an extended period of time, and so the concept of humiliation the anarchists entertain is not particularly interesting. Humiliation, according to the anarchist view, is based quite simply on people being what they are, namely, social beings—that is, creatures who need a stable society, which is a society with institutions. Thus the anarchist view is that people are humiliated by the very fact that they are social beings. In other words, people are humiliated because they are what they are, and not angels or solitary animals.

One can reply to the anarchist by saying that the fact that people are social beings is not a human artifact. Even if a particular person's membership in a particular society may be a human artifact—brought about by that very person—the fact that she lives in some sort of society is a fact of nature, like the shape of her body. Therefore the fact that human beings live in a society should not be seen as humiliating, even if a necessary condition for the existence of a society is the presence of institutions. The mere existence of these institutions is not a reason for people to consider themselves humiliated, since they are necessary for human existence owing to its very nature. This is in contrast to other institutions that are not essential for human existence, which do have humiliating potential.

The concept of humiliation we have associated with anarchism is thus encroachment on the individual's autonomy. In the present context this means institutional intervention that threatens to upset the individual's order of priorities, which expresses his selfhood. One reply to this anarchist view is that even if institutions are liable to distort individuals' order of priorities, including those which seem to them to be expressive of their individuality, these institutions may be doing so for the sake of the individuals' own interests. And if the institutions are actually protecting people's interests, even if the cost is a distortion of their (subjective) preferences, the individuals have no right to consider this a sound reason for feeling humiliated. The answer to this last argument is well known: individuals have a right to make mistakes in choosing what is best for them. Paternalism, which pretends to speak in the name of the individual's true interests, is especially humiliating. The sense in which paternalism is humiliating is that people are being treated as immature.

Returning to the anarchist view, we see that it is based

on a concept of humiliation even stronger than diminution of the individual's autonomy, namely, encroachment
on the individual's sovereignty. This latter concept of humiliation fits the arguments of anarchism as a historical
ideological trend, and not only as a fictional construction.
Permanent social institutions—those William Godwin calls
"positive institutions"—are humiliating by their very nature because they curb the sovereignty of individuals.
Only the individual is worthy of being the bearer of sovereignty.

In the anarchist view all governing institutions, including representative democracy, are humiliating because
they take away individual sovereignty in favor of those
who are supposed to be their representatives. Only the
individuals' direct, explicit agreement to an institutional
setup can possibly be reconciled with their sovereignty.
Anarchists, as Oscar Wilde points out, do not distinguish
between rule by kings and rule by the masses—both types
of rule are considered humiliating because both diminish
the individual's sovereignty. The anarchists' decent society
is therefore a generalized aristocracy, since each of its
members is sovereign.

Sovereignty is a familiar concept when writ large—that
is, when applied to a group of people or to a person at
the head of a collective, such as a monarch. This is also
the primary context in which we identify humiliation as a
blatant offense to sovereignty. When airplanes penetrate
the sovereign airspace of a neighbor state, deliberately
sounding a sonic boom over its cities—as, for example,
Israel and Syria have done to each other in the past—the
act is interpreted as a humiliation of the rival state. In the
anarchist's view sovereignty writ large is not sovereignty

at all, but it is handy for illustrating the valid idea of the sovereignty of individuals.

The sovereignty of individuals means their supreme right to act out of complete authority in any matter concerning them. Anarchists do, of course, qualify the individual's authority by some version of the harm principle—in other words, that no harm should be done to the sovereignty of other individuals. But the idea is clear: sovereignty rests only with the individual, and no institution can encroach upon the authority of individuals without humiliating them. Authoritarian institutions—that is, ones which are not based on direct agreement for a specific purpose—are humiliating by their very nature, since they take away the individual's sovereignty, or at least diminish it.

I began this section with a presentation of ideological anarchism and the skeptical challenge it poses for the idea of a decent society as a society with nonhumiliating institutions. The anarchist claim is that permanent ruling institutions are always humiliating, and so it is impossible for a decent society to exist. It seems that the skeptical claim carries weight only if skeptical anarchism is supported by political anarchism—that is, by a proposal for organizing society without permanent institutions. For if it is impossible in principle for a stable human society to exist without such institutions, then people are humiliated by the very conditions of human existence, since these conditions include the existence of such institutions. Being humiliated by the need for institutions would then be comparable to being humiliated by the fact that human existence requires people to attend to their bodily functions. Functions are functions and they are a necessity that knows no law. Similarly, vital institutions are vital institutions and they too are an irreproachable necessity. Humiliation is, after all, injury to self-respect, that is, to the respect a human being deserves for the very fact of being human, and so it is not fitting to consider anything vital for human existence to be humiliating.

Thus the force of the skeptical anarchist challenge depends upon the anarchist's ability to offer a proposal for a stable human society without permanent governing institutions. This is not a demand for presenting a utopian society without institutions. Such a demand would be unfair, since anarchism rejects the despotism of a utopia as a fixed life-setup, because it sins against the open-endedness of life. We are not even asking the political anarchist to present a proposal for achieving a society without institutions, since any proposal of this sort is suspect to anarchists for the same reason that they reject utopias. The only demand being made of anarchists is that they show how a society without governing institutions can be possible. An anarchist utopia, such as the one William Morris presents in *News from Nowhere*,[2] can be helpful in demonstrating how a society without institutions may be possible even if the chances of realizing it are minuscule.

Two main types of anarchism can be distinguished: communal anarchism and anarchism as a "union of egoists," to use Max Stirner's phrase.[3] These two types of anarchism would respond differently to the challenge of a decent society as a society without permanent governing institutions. Communal anarchists might claim that a society without institutions is possible, but only at the cost of exchanging what Plato calls a "refined society" for a "healthy society" (*Republic* 372–373). In other words, a society without institutions is possible within the setting of primary relationships—in a small, intimate society, such as a voluntary commune. Such a society cannot guarantee the standard of living of modern developed societies that enjoy the advantages of scale, division of labor, and specialized professionalism. It can, however, be a decent society that protects the individual from the humiliation involved in dealing with permanent ruling institutions. Human dignity, says the anarchist, is not for sale, so there is no point in assessing the price of a decent but undeveloped society in economic terms.

As against this anarchist version of the decent society it may be claimed that giving up a decent standard of living entails giving up the conditions of honorable human existence. The conditions of decent existence—what is perceived as human dignity—constitute a relative concept dependent on society and history. Giving up economic advantages for the sake of a "healthy society" in a commune without institutions is perceived in developed societies as a nonhonorable lowering of one's standard of living. In other words, a Tolstoyan commune may be a nonhumiliating society by virtue of the fact that it contains no permanent ruling institutions, but it is not a decent society insofar as its living conditions of grinding poverty are perceived as humiliating.

One of the goals of the "union of egoists" type of anarchism in abolishing all governing institutions is to guarantee everyone the highest possible standard of living through a market free of institutional limitations. The market is considered a free association of producers and consumers, where the sovereignty of individuals lies precisely in their being free producers and consumers. Thus humiliation is any institutional interference with individuals' economic sovereignty, such as taxation. Radical anarchists of the egoistic type do not recognize the existence of goods and services that are generally considered public goods—services such as street lighting, for example, that cannot be efficiently guaranteed without compulsory institutional intervention, as otherwise they will be taken advantage of by free riders. Egoistic anarchists believe that the market can solve this problem even for services such as defense forces and the legal system, not to speak of street lighting.[4] In short, they believe there can be a pure market society without any political framework—that is, without any humiliating institutions. The egoistic anarchists' solution to the problem of the decent society is the market economy, free of political institutions, yet including economic organizations. The market society guarantees a decent society without humiliating institutions for the simple reason that there aren't any governing institutions at all.

One immediate retort to the idea that a market society without governing institutions is a decent society is that a market society includes economic organizations, particularly monopolies and cartels, which are in fact governing institutions. The coercive power of monopolies is no less than that of political institutions. Thus the idea that a market society is free of institutions that have the power to humiliate people is a fairy tale—especially if the society has the task of supplying security, as well as an efficient legal system, through the workings of the market. The companies providing such protection would be like mobsters' debt-collectors who make offers "that can't be refused."

But there is something outlandish about the idea of a market society as a decent society: in a democratic society political institutions are justified precisely by the fact that they are meant to protect the members of the society from humiliations generated by the market society. This includes safeguards against poverty, homelessness, exploitation, degrading work conditions, and the unavailability of education and health services for those "sovereign consumers" who are unable to pay for them. In developed societies, the market society is the problem rather than the solution.

If the market society is supposed to provide an anarchist solution to the problem of building a society without institutions that does not involve giving up a human standard of living, these two responses show that the market society cannot do away with coercive institutions and cannot provide a humane standard of living for all. We must keep these arguments in mind, but we must also keep in mind the skeptical anarchist argument that no society with permanent governing institutions is a decent one.

Stoicism: There Is No Humiliating Society

The polar opposite of the anarchist view is the "Stoic" view that no society can provide sound reasons for feeling humiliated. Since no external reason can be a sound reason for such a feeling, there are no societies that are not decent ones.

In the anarchist view, as we have seen, it is breaches of the individual's autonomy and, even more so, of the individual's sovereignty, that are humiliating. The key Stoic term analogous to autonomy is 'autarchy.' Autarchy—the ability to be self-sufficient in satisfying one's needs—is a capacity concept, whereas autonomy requires opportunity as well as capacity. In other words, autarchy does not require specific environmental conditions for its satisfaction. Environmental conditions are a matter of (moral) luck, and a person's autonomy cannot be judged in matters over which one has no control. External life conditions are usually not under one's control, but autarchy, conceived as spiritual autonomy, can be achieved even under the most extreme external conditions, such as slavery. Slaves can hide their thoughts from their master and so the master does not have possession of the slave's thoughts. Epictetus the slave could thus have as much spiritual autonomy as the emperor Marcus Aurelius. Since thought is the essential predicate of a human being, it is autonomy of thought rather than physical liberty that is the highest expression of autarchy.

Humiliation is thus the breach of a person's autarchy, and this occurs only when one is not autonomous in one's thoughts—for example, when one is swayed by emotion. Individuals are not autarchic when their view of the world does not permit them to distinguish between what is good in and of itself and what is valueless or has value only as an instrument for achieving something which does have intrinsic value. Thus, for example, honor, money, and even health do not possess intrinsic value, and one should feel equanimity about them. This doesn't mean that you should be indifferent about your health just because it has only instrumental value, but you shouldn't get terribly excited about it in the sense of being in an emotional state with no rational justification. Stoic apathy is not the absence of feeling, but the admission only of rationally justified emotions. People lose their autarchy when, under the influence of their surroundings, they adopt a mistaken view of the true value of things in the world.

A society is not decent if it contributes to its members' lack of autarchy, but society cannot obstruct the path of people who are absolutely determined to live autarchic lives. In this sense society is ultimately unable to humiliate anyone who does not want to be humiliated. A rational person cannot be humiliated, because one's social environment cannot provide a sound reason for this. Anyone who does not realize that he is not subject to others is merely "a corpse and a gallon of blood," says Epictetus, graphically expressing the Stoic sentiment.

The questions raised by the version of Stoicism described here are the following: If humiliation is injury to your self-respect, then why should any external behavior toward you justify your feeling humiliated? Honor is, of course, something that is bestowed on people by society. But, in contrast to social honor, self-respect is the honor persons bestow upon themselves by virtue of their own humanity. Why then should your self-respect be determined or influenced by what others think about you or the way they act toward you? In particular, why should the way one is treated by anonymous social institutions affect the self-respect of persons who are autarchic in their thoughts? Why should other people's recognition be important to one's self-respect? After all, we are not talking about a person's self-esteem, which must be validated through interaction with others. Self-respect, in contrast to self-esteem, is the honor a person grants herself solely on the basis of the awareness that she is human. So why should it be affected by the evaluation of others? Moreover, self-respect, as the term itself implies, is respect that depends upon the person's own self. In order to acquire self-respect one does not need any external authorization in the form of appreciation or recognition. Therefore no society nor any members of society are capable of affording sound reasons for feeling humiliated.

The Stoic challenge to the enterprise of delineating the decent society is central to the entire enterprise. We will be able to take up this challenge only after further explicating the concepts of self-respect and humiliation. Here I will make do with a few critical comments on the Stoic argument, following Nietzsche.

Ignoring the need for recognition by others in the process of acquiring self-respect is based, as Nietzsche pointed out, on resentment of the other rather than on the sublime freedom inherent in self-affirmation: ". . . slave morality from the outset says No to what is 'outside', what is 'different', what is 'not itself.'"[5] The claim is thus that the slave's so-called autarchy in denying the importance of the "outside" for determining one's attitudes is actually a defense mechanism of resentful slaves who want to avenge themselves on their surroundings. In other words, it is impossible for anyone of inferior social status to be truly immune to external humiliation. Self-respect requires social confidence, and the lack of this confidence leads to a false independence that is the essence of slave morality. It is the basic social confidence of aristocrats that enables them to truly ignore the opinions of others and achieve a self-affirmation independent of the others' attitudes. Slaves are not capable of this. Nietzsche is prepared to go even further and consider the possibility that "even supposing that the affect of contempt, of looking down from a superior height, *falsifies* the image of that which it despises, it will at any rate still be a much less serious falsification than that perpetrated on its opponent—*in effigie* of course—by the submerged hatred, the vengefulness of the impotent."[6]

The Stoic transition from "political man" to "internal man," who is immune to society's attitude toward his humanity, is not a real option in Nietzsche's view. People of inferior social status ("slaves") are psychologically incapable of extricating themselves from humiliation simply by declaring that the humiliating master is "outside" their inner world. The inner world of the slave includes the master within itself. "Slave morality" is the result of this vengeful internalization. The end result of slave morality is the Christian view that turns humiliation into a formative experience fostering humility. The Christian attitude toward humiliation is a continuation of the Stoic attitude by other means—perverse means, to be sure, in Nietzsche's view—which turn humiliation into an instrument for training saints. The Christian saint is intended to be the heir of the Stoic wise man, but there is a marked difference between the Christian truly humble man and the Stoic "internal" man. The Christian humble person is supposed to pay no regard to himself while being constantly preoccupied with himself, especially with the purity of his own motives. This seems to be a logical impossibility. In contrast, the Stoic "internal" man is supposed to ignore the outside social world—not an easy task, but not a logical impossibility.

Nietzsche does indeed believe that there is a difference between the Stoic and the Christian views in the way they evaluate humiliation. The Stoic sage, whose thoughts are free, is truly capable of such reevaluation—that is, of seeing himself as free and as not humiliated by his master—whereas the Christian, in Nietzsche's view, is not truly capable of it. This is because the Christian is full of *ressentiment*. He may be capable of "loving" even the humiliator who strikes his cheek, but he also makes sure to inwardly send the perpetrator to hell. Hell is the resentment-saturated revenge of the humiliated Christian.

I began this chapter with two opposite views questioning the enterprise of characterizing the decent society as a society whose institutions do not humiliate people. The view at one end of the spectrum claims that there cannot be nonhumiliating social institutions. The view at the opposite end claims that no social institutions are humiliating, and so in this sense there is no nondecent society. We must now navigate between the anarchist Scylla and the Stoic Charybdis, tied to the mast of the ship, resisting the seductive singing of the sirens from both ends of the spectrum.

2

Rights

A decent society might alternatively be defined as one that does not violate the rights of people dependent on it. The idea is that only a society with a notion of rights can have the concepts of self-respect and humiliation required for a decent society. The enterprise of a decent society thus has meaning only relative to a society with a clear notion of rights.

I will examine this suggestion in the light of two questions:

1. Is the concept of rights a necessary condition for forming the concepts of respect and humiliation required for characterizing decent and nondecent societies?
2. Which rights, if any, have to be honored by the institutions of a society for it to be considered a decent one? Is the honoring of all rights a sufficient condition for considering a society decent?

I began this book with the claim that a society cannot be called decent if its institutions afford good reasons for people dependent on them to consider themselves humiliated. And what better reason can you have for feeling humiliated than the violation of your rights, especially those rights that are supposed to protect your dignity? The force of this last claim stems from its air of obviousness: "What better reason for feeling humiliated could there be than the violation of rights?" But this particular air of obviousness indicates what Wittgenstein calls "being held in the grip of a picture." It is a case in which a model of reality is perceived as reality itself, simply because we cannot imagine any alternative to that model. To loosen the grip of the picture, an alternative must be offered.

One alternative is a society founded on a strict notion of duty, but without the concept of rights. The question then is whether such a duty-based society is capable of forming a concept of humiliation. Such a society could denounce certain types of behavior as humiliating. It could also recognize other types of behavior as respectful of human beings as such, and require its members to act respectfully toward one another as a social obligation. So far there is no problem. The society's system of duties defines what sorts of behavior on the part of those held liable to these duties are considered respectful or humiliating. Institutions that do not fulfill their obligations of granting appropriate respect are perceived as behaving in a humiliating manner, thus removing the society they are in from the ranks of decent societies.

If it is all that simple, then why do we need to ask whether a society without a notion of rights can be a decent one? But there actually is a difficulty, as it would seem that in a duty-based society humiliating behavior does not provide its victims with a sound reason for feeling humiliated. By assumption, the victims do not have the right to be protected from humiliation. People who violate the society's prohibitions on humiliating behavior are not sinning specifically against the victim to any greater extent than against anyone else. Their transgression is a violation of the society's prohibitions rather than of anyone's rights. Paradoxically, in a duty-based society people can act in a humiliating way but no one can be humiliated.

Imagine a duty-based society that commands its young people to respect old people, say by standing up and giving them a seat on a bus. Old people are not considered to have the right to a seat, but the young have the duty to give them their seats. Imagine now that the bus driver is under the obligation to make sure that the behavior on his bus conforms with the society's norms. In such a case, a particular old man who points out to the bus driver that he is being prevented from sitting down by a teenager who refuses to give up his seat does not have a preferred status over any other passenger on the bus who points out this state of affairs to the driver. It is true that the respect due to the old has been denied on the bus, but the particular old man for whom no one has stood up is not considered to have been treated with disrespect. The expression "respect-for-the-elderly" is an unbreakable (syncategorematic) combination, just as the expression "lily-livered" cannot be decomposed into a lily and a liver.

Is it true, then, that a duty-based society does not provide sound reasons for the victims of humiliating behavior to consider themselves humiliated? I don't believe so. We have assumed that in a duty-based society humiliation is forbidden. Thus anyone in such a society can recognize humiliating behavior for what it is—humiliating. The question is whether a victim of such behavior has a good reason for feeling humiliated. He obviously may be caused to feel that way, but does he have a reason for it if he lacks the idea that his rights have been violated? The combination of a reason for considering a particular behavior humiliating, added to the fact that this behavior is causing humiliation in the person at whom it is directed, gives the victim a sound reason and not only a cause for considering himself humiliated. A reason is a justification for having a specific feeling if it consists of a general reason for having that sort of feeling, combined with a particular cause for feeling that way in the present case. The old man for whom no one stood up is not just any passenger. He is not just an observer of behavior lacking in respect-for-the-elderly. Since it was his own old age that was treated with disrespect, the teenager who treated him this way afforded him with a reason and not only a cause for feeling humiliated.

It is entirely possible that this particular old man did not actually feel humiliated—perhaps he was secretly pleased to think that no one had noticed how old he was, and that he still looked young enough to stand on the bus—but that an old woman on the same bus, who had a place to sit, not only felt that the teenager on the bus had been negligent but also felt that her own old age had been slighted. Should we then say that she has a reason and not only a cause for feeling slighted? After all, there is a general reason here for feeling offended, and this reason is also a cause of the old woman's particular feeling of being offended. Then isn't this also a reason for her to feel offended? True, the old woman has a reason for feeling the respect due to her old age to be slighted because the teenager did not give his seat to the old man, even though she herself does have a place to sit. But her reason is not as good as that of the direct victim of the behavior, since she is only an affronted observer and not a victim herself.

There is something a trifle comic in the description of the old woman feeling offended by the insult to the old man. The scene depicted may give the impression that the issue it raises is trifling. But a rather important issue is actually implicit in the story of the affronted old woman. Humiliation, like embarrassment, is contagious. It is an emotion we may feel as a result of mere identification with others even if we are not the direct victims of the humiliating behavior. If we identify with the victim in that we share the characteristic for which he is being humiliated, then we also have a justified reason for feeling ourselves humiliated. This issue is discussed in more detail later on.

Duty morality stresses the claim that the humiliated or insulted person does not have any special standing with respect to the person who has injured her. Anyone can challenge the humiliator with the argument that humiliation is an offense against the explicit duty of "Thou shalt not humiliate." The question is whether this duty can be justified without smuggling in the concept of rights through the back door. It may be argued that this duty can be justified only by referring to the fact that humiliation is a painful injury to the interests of the victim. Although duty morality addresses its demands to its moral agents only through the use of the language of duty, the justification for these demands, which does not appear explicitly in the demands themselves, may require the concept of rights.

I see the force of the claim that duty morality cannot work without implicitly making use of the concept of rights, but it still seems doubtful to me that this concept plays a mandatory role in the justification of the duty not to humiliate. An analogy may clarify the issue. We may assume that a humanistic duty morality will include the duty to avoid cruelty to animals. I do not think that we need the concept of animal rights in order to justify this duty. It may well be justified by what cruelty says about those who practice it and the society that allows them to do so. Such a justification need not involve animal rights at all, although it will probably involve the fact that animals can feel pain. The same may be true of humiliation in a duty morality. Justifying the duty not to humiliate undoubtedly involves the fact that humiliation causes the victim pain and suffering. It may also involve the victim's clear interest in not being humiliated. But in order to claim that the justification relies on the concept of rights it is not enough to note the victim's interest—it is also necessary to show that this interest is a good thing in itself. A duty morality may be based on the idea that the thing which is good in itself is the absence of humiliation, while fulfilling the victim's interests is only a means to this end. In such a case the duty not to humiliate in a duty society would not require the concept of rights.

The conclusion to be drawn here, then, is that a society whose morality is based on duty, without a correlative notion of rights, not only can have a concept of humiliation but can also provide sound reasons for feeling humiliated.

A society based on a morality of ends, even if it lacks the notions of both duty and rights, can also provide us with a backdrop for explicating the concept of nonhumiliation required for characterizing the decent society. It should be made clear from the outset that specifying a particular society's morality by means of one key notion, such as duty, ends, or rights, generally does not necessarily imply that the society lacks the other notions. Thus Kant believes that we can achieve the end of honoring people's humanity through the absolute obligation of the categorical imperative. Characterizing a particular morality through one central concept is intended to stress the explanatory primacy of that concept over all others. For example, in a duty morality the concept of duty plays an essential role in the explanation of the concept of rights, rather than the other way around. But in the present context, when I characterize a particular morality through a central concept I actually mean to imply that the morality does not contain the other concepts at all. Thus when I use the expression "duty morality," I mean that the concept of duty is the only moral concept at its disposal, and that it does not include the concept of rights at all. And when I speak about a "morality of ends," I am assuming that this morality does not include the concepts of rights and obligations.

A morality of ends is based on a vision of the place of creatures in the chain of being. Man is the "crown of creation," that is, a creature who must be treated in a special way because of what he is. Any treatment that does not accord Man his special place in the chain of being constitutes humiliation. This sort of morality is based not on duties or commandments but on the personal example of an individual who epitomizes it. People who humiliate others in a society based on this sort of morality are not reproved for having violated the victims' rights or for failing to fulfill a duty. Rather, they are reproved for not having acted the way the exemplary person would have done. Albert Schweitzer would not have acted like that, someone might say to the transgressor. Such a society can clearly have a well-developed notion of humiliation. Victims of humiliating behavior in this sort of society also have a reason for feeling humiliated. Again, this is not because of any particular right of theirs, but because they have been treated as lesser beings. In short, the arguments about humiliation in a society based on a morality of ends are exactly parallel to those in a duty-based society.

Self-Respect: The Case of Uncle Tom

A popular example of a good man lacking self-respect is Uncle Tom.[1] Uncle Tom has become the negative symbol of the movement whose goal is restoring human dignity to black people. For this movement Uncle Tom is an example of the biblical slave who says "I love my master" and whose ear must be pierced. Even if there is something heartening about Uncle Tom's sense of faithfulness, it seems easy to interpret it as the faithfulness of a dog to its master. What is missing is a sense of self-respect.

The story of Uncle Tom can be told in various ways for various purposes. What is important for the purpose of clarifying the relationship between self-respect and rights is the distinction between two issues that can be exemplified through this story. One issue is the total absence of the notion of rights; the other is the inability to demand one's rights. A possible argument in favor of an internal

relationship between rights and self-respect is that humiliation does not mean that one's rights have been violated,
but rather that one is incapable of demanding them.
Uncle Tom can be described as being aware of the violation of his basic rights but incapable of effectively demanding that they be honored. In his case, however, standing
on his rights in the sense of an explicit demand is liable
to endanger both him and his family. So the minimal
requirement for standing on one's rights is that the victim
should at least feel indignation toward the people who are
trampling them. The victim is expected at least not to
acquiesce to the evil and the evildoer. In this sense Uncle
Tom is perceived as someone who does acquiesce even
though he is aware of what is happening. Such acquies-
cence is psychological acceptance, and the claim is that
someone who reacts this way lacks self-respect.

Yet there is another reading of the Uncle Tom story—a
religious reading. Uncle Tom doesn't have a concept of
rights, but he has deep religious convictions which tell
him that all people, whether black or white, are descended
from Adam, who was created in God's image. Thus Tom's
human dignity lies in his family tree going back to Adam.
Tom does not translate this fact into terms of rights, such
as his right of inheritance as one of Adam's children. But
he is fully aware that his honor as a child of Adam is no
less than the honor that must be accorded any human
being. At the same time, Uncle Tom submissively accepts
whatever his masters require of him, believing that this is
God's will and that he is being tested. Questioning the
established order would be a manifestation of pride,
which is a greater sin than that of his abusers. Rebellion
is wrong, because only God can redeem the oppressed.

Does Uncle Tom's worldview, so saturated with religious innocence, lack the concept of self-respect? Is it a worldview without a concept of humiliation? My claim is that there is no difficulty in pinning down Tom's notion of humiliation. His master treats him in a way unfitting for a child of Adam, their common ancestor. Tom believes that this is not the way to treat someone created in God's image. The question thus is not whether a person lacking the concept of rights can have a concept of humiliation. The really difficult question, again, is whether Tom, in spite of lacking a concept of rights, can have a reason for feeling humiliated which we would consider sound. Moreover, if we do not believe that the world was created by God, can we still consider Tom's reason a justification for feeling humiliated?

Joel Feinberg believes that there can be no idea of self-respect which is not tied to the concept of rights.[2] Or rather, he believes that without the concept of rights there can be no idea of self-respect which *we* would deem justified, and analogously there can be no concept of humiliation which *we* would consider justified. We are not interested in reasons that Uncle Tom himself would consider justified but ones that seem justified to us. "Us" here includes all those who base their conception of morality on the humanistic assumption that the only justification for morality is human. I thus understand Feinberg's challenge as questioning whether someone with a humanistic conception of morality is capable of having a concept of self-respect or humiliation without a concept of rights, and that question I have already answered in the affirmative. Both a duty morality and a morality of ends can provide the ground for cultivating the concepts of self-respect and humiliation.

But even within the context of a morality of rights

Uncle Tom presents a challenge. Rights are interests—interests of a particular kind, but interests nonetheless. And whatever the nature of these interests, respecting persons means giving the appropriate weight to their interests, or at least to their interests of the appropriate sort. People's concern about the respect given them is in part a concern about having their interests respected, so that they can be fulfilled and protected. Uncle Tom is a person with interests, but he seems lacking in concern for these interests. The question then is how a person can have self-respect if he is unconcerned about his interests.

At first glance there seems to be a paradox here. If an interest is an issue of concern to an individual, how is it (logically) possible for a person to be unconcerned about what concerns him? But this paradox is only apparent. The question of how someone can be unconcerned about his concerns is unreal because concerns are issues that people *should* be concerned about, but not necessarily issues that they actually *are* concerned about. Concerns must not be identified with preferences, and when the two are distinguished the paradox vanishes. What remains is only the problem of how people can have self-respect if they are unconcerned about issues which they ought to be concerned about. Such people seem unconcerned about the main issues relating to their concerns, which is that their interests should be respected. Anyone who lacks this sort of second-order interest is lacking in self-respect.

Judging Uncle Tom humanistically would lead us to say that he lacks self-respect. But describing him as a religious believer portrays a man with considerable dignity. What should we give up: the humanistic assumption, or the idea that Uncle Tom has dignity in spite of his servility?

Describing Uncle Tom's impressive Christian inner world is like describing the inner world of a slave who is a Stoic sage. The Stoic "inner" world and the Christian "inner" world are both strategies for preserving dignity under harsh conditions. But these are *substitutes* which must not be used as a basis for a decent society.

Rights as a Sufficient Condition for Respect

Which rights, if any, can constitute a sufficient condition for self-respect, or for what may be called dignity? Putting it differently, the violation of which rights provides a sufficient condition for humiliation?

Human rights are the natural candidates for the requirement of sufficiency. These are moral rights—that is, rights whose justification has a moral character. Rights are interests, and when these interests are good in and of themselves the rights are moral ones. Human rights are those possessed equally by all people solely by virtue of their humanity. The justification for human rights is that they are meant to protect human dignity. To be sure, there have been attempts to justify human rights in other ways. For example, one way is to see them as a minimal condition for people's freedom of action, without which they could not be considered moral agents. But if that justification is used, then human rights are not being considered a good thing in and of themselves, but only an essential means for something else which *is* inherently good—namely, being moral agents. In contrast, if human rights are justified directly as an interest constituting human dignity, then these rights are seen as good in and of themselves. In the present view, human rights are considered a protection for human dignity. Human rights are "symptoms"—in the context of a morality of rights—for identifying human dignity.

What would we say about a society that respects human rights but violates other rights of the people in the society, such as their civil rights? Could such a society be considered a decent one? Let us use the example of civil rights to explore this question. The general right to be a citizen is a human right, but this does not necessarily imply one's right to be a citizen in the particular society in which one happens to be living. A society which takes away the citizenship of a person who has a right to be a citizen of that society is violating that person's human rights. Our question, however, is about a society that doesn't take away people's citizenship but tramples on their civil rights. An example of a civil right that is not a human right is the right to vote. Withholding this right from women (as Switzerland did until quite recently) is an act unworthy of a decent society. Not giving women the right to vote means treating them as nonadults and therefore as not fully human.

Different societies represent different ways of being human. Violation of civil rights is liable to do significant harm to people's ability to express their humanity as it is shaped by that society, and thus constitutes humiliation. For this reason the fact that a given society honors people's human rights cannot be considered a sufficient condition for its being a decent society, since that society might well humiliate its members as citizens even though it does not violate their human rights.

3

Honor

A decent society is a nonhumiliating one. But what term do we use to contrast with humiliation? So far we have been using 'self-respect' as the opposite of 'humiliation.' Not only is the meaning of self-respect far from clear, but there are also a number of competing concepts for delineating the decent society. Let us try to find the proper concept to contrast with humiliation from among these competing ones.

One of these concepts requires a preliminary discussion. This is the concept of honor, in the ordinary sense of the term. The suggestion is that the decent society is a society in which every person is accorded due honor. Since I am limiting the concept of the decent society to the behavior of its institutions, a decent society would then be one whose institutions accord all people their due honor. My intention here is to rehabilitate the idea of honor in political discussions, rather than considering it a mere relic from the past. But in that case, why not define the decent society directly in terms of honor?

Two senses of the expression "due honor" must be distinguished. One refers to the distribution of honor, and the question is whether all people get their fair share of honor. The other sense of "due honor" refers to our assessment of such honor in our own eyes, and the question is whether it is given for worthwhile acts. For example, a warrior society may extend due honor to its warriors, in the sense that it does not deprive anyone who has contributed to its wars of his fair share of honor. Each warrior is allotted honor in proportion to his contribution. The honor due to warriors is not bestowed on those who did not fight its wars. There are no medal-encrusted troop-reviewing generals who never smelled gunpowder or took part in a battle. Such a society accords everyone due honor, but this does not mean that the concept of honor in that society is a worthy one in our eyes. On the contrary, we may consider it utterly perverse. A society which appropriately shares what is not worthy of honoring is like a group of gangsters who share their booty in a fair and friendly way. The sharing is fair, but the booty is morally worthless.

In general we are concerned with the question of whether a society distributes (worthwhile) honor to those who deserve it—that is, whether appropriate honor is distributed justly. But concern with the just distribution of honor belongs to the just society rather than the decent society. The concept of social honor that is available for distribution is a graded concept. Social honor given equally to everyone would be empty.

A society with an unjust distribution of social honor is not necessarily a nondecent one. The concept of honor involved in our discussion of the decent society—the one whose injury constitutes humiliation—is not a graded concept. It must be granted to everyone equally because of what they are and not because of what they have done.

An unjust distribution of (worthwhile) social honor is indeed an injustice. But this does not mean that a society with such an unjust distribution of honor is not a decent one.

Thus the concept of honor needed at the basis of the decent society is not the notion of social honor. The concept of humiliation that would disqualify a society from being a decent one cannot be the lack of social honor. If we want to base the decent society on the concept of the honor that everyone deserves in equal measure, we must move from social honor to human dignity. From the viewpoint of those conferring such honor we speak of respect for humans, while from the viewpoint of those honored we speak of dignity. Yet understanding the concept of dignity requires an understanding of the notion of social honor as well.

The concept of social honor is important to our discussion of the decent society because the concept of human dignity evolved historically out of the idea of social honor. The idea of human dignity is a relative latecomer. The word "dignity" comes from the Latin *dignitas,* which means social honor. Analogously, the concept of humiliation as injury to human dignity evolved from the concept of social humiliation. Social honor is thus prior to intrinsic honor, but the priority is only historical, not conceptual: the concept of social honor is not logically necessary for explaining the concept of human dignity. The priority consists in the fact that one concept evolved from the other, in the way that the Hebrew word for honor or respect, *kavod,* evolved from the adjective *kaved,* meaning heavy (with possessions).

In sum, the concept of honor that is relevant to the

decent society is the concept of human dignity. This is a type of honor that people ought to have, and its violation is a reason to consider oneself humiliated. But what is meant here by humiliation—do we mean a violation of self-respect, or a diminution of self-esteem, or a breach of integrity, or just an injury to human dignity? All of these are candidates for the concept of honor whose violation constitutes a reason for persons to consider themselves humiliated.

Self-Respect and Self-Esteem

The first pair of concepts to be examined are self-respect and self-esteem. These concepts can and should be distinguished in connection with the decent society.[1] The association between the two is causal rather than conceptual. One reason it is important to distinguish them is that respect constitutes a ground for treating people equally, while esteem forms a basis for ranking people. A variety of moral theories tell us that we ought to respect people purely on the basis of their humanity, but no moral theory tells us that we ought to esteem people simply because they are human.

Can one have self-respect without self-esteem, and, conversely, can one have self-esteem without self-respect? Cases in which people have self-esteem—even very great self-esteem—but lack self-respect are relatively easy to find: we are familiar with people who value themselves very highly on the basis of their achievements, but are nevertheless ready to grovel before anyone in a position of power who might be able to do something for them. Groveling is a form of flattery in which a person acts servilely to others in order to give them a false feeling of superiority, thus advancing the groveler's interests. Grovelers humiliate themselves in order to achieve other advantages at the cost of their self-respect—advantages that may well serve their self-esteem. The actor Högen, who sold his soul to the (Nazi) devil in István Szabo's film "Mephisto," is one example. (The character of Högen is based on Klaus Mann's description of his uncle Gustav Grundgens, a noted German actor.) Richard Wagner in real life is perhaps another example. If one is interested, as I am, in institutional humiliation, and analogously in manifestations of human dignity vis-á-vis institutions, then groveling is a form of behavior deserving of attention, since it is typically performed toward people in positions of power. Thus the groveler, who lacks self-respect but has great self-esteem, is a figure we have no difficulty imagining or identifying.

In order to show that self-esteem and self-respect are independent in the converse direction as well, we must find a case in which a person lacks self-esteem yet possesses self-respect. This is a less familiar situation. A person can have low self-esteem because she doesn't value her achievements, yet nevertheless retain her sense of self-respect. Such a person may be aware that her achievements are valued by others, but she is so hard on herself that she is unable to esteem herself. In the case of such a perfectionist we are entitled to suspect that deep within herself she not only values herself as much as she ought to, but considerably more than she ought to. Yet this psychological suspicion does not detract from the conceptual possibility that such a case might exist. The figure described here is psychologically possible. A person can lack self-esteem—in spite of proven achievements—yet possess uncompromising self-respect. This self-respect may be expressed in stubborn insistence on one's basic rights, or in a mad refusal to compromise one's personal honesty in the style of Michael Kohlhass (the hero of a story by Heinrich von Kleist), or in readiness to endanger oneself in a struggle against people who insult or humiliate one, even if they are stronger than oneself.

There is no contradiction between this claim and the one at the beginning of this book, where I suggested that there could be a Czech Republic in which people might gain more self-respect but lose their self-esteem. They could easily find themselves in a position of losing their self-esteem because they lack a useful role in the new economic and social order, yet they would no longer be forced to compromise their integrity and self-respect, as was the case under the old regime. The issue is not whether the present description is correct but whether it is free of contradictions. I believe it is.

The claim that self-esteem is a ranking concept relies on the beliefs people have about their own achievements. But achievements are the result of effort, while a person's self-esteem can be supported by traits that do not require any effort. For example, members of the nobility may base their self-esteem on the fact that they are of noble birth. Thus even if achievement ought to be related to effort from a moral point of view, this is not a conceptual requirement. I do not believe that members of the nobility constitute a problem for the idea that there is a connection between self-esteem and achievement, since self-esteem may be based not only on actual achievements but also on a belief in one's ability to achieve. Members of the nobility consider their noble birth a reason for self-esteem because they believe that their family tree, which they see as adorned with glorious achievements, guarantees that they too are born for great deeds. Their self-esteem does not depend merely on the fact that they were born who they were.

I have been claiming that self-esteem is based on ranking traits, while self-respect may be based on other traits. But is this true? Both the esteem and the respect are provided for the self by the self. But one's selfhood, or individuality—the fact that one has one's own judgment, one's own preferences, one's own principles—is itself an achievement, not a given. One's selfhood is the result of a process—a never-ending process that is not always successful. The button-molder in Ibsen's *Peer Gynt*, Canetti's man of the crowd, are creatures devoid of individuality. How can self-respect be based on traits of belonging rather than achievement if one's very individuality is the result of a rankable achievement? The answer is that the ability to be an individual is not necessarily the trait for which people ought to be respected. Even if we accept the idea that individuality is an achievement required for self-respect, it is not necessarily the trait which justifies self-respect.

At any rate, I intend to demonstrate that the trait which does justify self-respect is primarily one of belonging and only secondarily one of achievement. An example of such a trait is belonging to a group which does not require anything other than being in the group, while being a prototypical member of the group is an achievement. Being Irish is a matter of belonging, but being a good Irishman is an achievement. A trait that justifies self-respect may be an achievement trait in a secondary sense, but it must be a belonging trait in its primary sense. A good Irishman believes that all the Irish are worthy of respect purely by virtue of being Irish. Moreover, he believes that all Irishmen ought to respect themselves for being Irish, even though only good Irishmen are capable of respecting themselves as Irishmen. A good Irishman, however, does not consider the fact that only good Irishmen can respect themselves as Irishmen as giving others permission to dishonor Irishmen who are not good Irishmen. The good Irishman in our example believes that good Irishmen deserve special honor to the extent that they are good Irishmen. The evaluation of good Irishmen is a ranking evaluation. But the basic respect that all Irishmen deserve because of being Irish is an egalitarian concept. If "Irishman" is replaced by "human being" everywhere in our example, the point I have been trying to make becomes clear.

Integrity

Another claim might be that a humiliating society is one whose institutions cause people to compromise their integrity. This is a society that corrupts the integrity of its people. Thus the contrast I intend to discuss now is between humiliation and integrity. It would seem that integrity, in distinction from self-respect, is a thick concept that one can dig one's teeth into. A person with integrity is someone who cannot be corrupted. A humiliating society is one which subjects people of integrity to blackmail and forces them to make despicable compromises. For example, only if you join the Party will your children be eligible to go to a "proper" school; only if you sign a petition against your colleague will you be able to keep your job.

I suggested that a person with integrity is someone who cannot be corrupted. But what sort of corruption is meant? Is it moral corruption? Is the relation between integrity and moral corruption a conceptual or an associative one? An example of a relation which is only associative and not conceptual is that between being a basketball player and being tall—you can be a basketball player without being tall. Similarly, a person with integrity is generally but not necessarily a moral person. A cold, calculating criminal, like Balzac's Vautrin, may be someone with integrity. Vautrin is not a civically or morally decent person, but he adheres firmly to his principle of uncompromising loyalty to his friends. Vautrin admittedly lives a double life of bourgeois respectability in the daytime and crime at night, but he does not therefore have a double standard. After all, John le Carré's Smiley also lives a double life as a secret agent, but his integrity is irreproachable. Adolf Eichmann was a devout Nazi who never compromised his despicable principles—it was absolutely impossible to bribe him. In contrast, his assistant Kurt Becher was corrupt and bribable. We can clearly say that Kurt Becher was corrupt, but can we say that Eichmann was a man of integrity? I believe that our hesitation about calling Eichmann a man of integrity stems not from any conceptual considerations but only from the strong connotation of the perverse nature of his principles.

But there is another possible interpretation of these phenomena. The difference between Eichmann and Vautrin may be that, even though Vautrin himself is not a moral person, the principles he is loyal to, because of which we consider him a person of integrity, are moral ones, such as faithfulness to friends, while the principles Eichmann adhered to are totally immoral. Thus although there is no conceptual relation between having integrity and being moral, there is one between the principles a person of integrity adheres to and the fact that these principles are moral. The fact that a person of integrity is loyal to moral principles, however, does not mean that he has moral considerations for adhering to these principles or that he applies them morally. A mobster who is faithful to his friends does not act this way out of moral considerations, even if his faithfulness is not based on fear of punishment by the Cosa Nostra.

Thus a society whose institutions cause its calculating criminals to abandon their integrity—for example, by informing on their associates—is not necessarily a nondecent society. It depends on what sort of means the society employs for this purpose. There is reason to suspect that if the criminals in a society are truly people with integrity, then their informing may be the result of improper means, such as torture—means that may prevent the society from being considered a decent one. If, however, the society compromises the integrity of its criminals by morally acceptable means, such as placing them in a "Prisoner's Dilemma" type of situation, this does not constitute humiliation.

In conclusion, if we were to define the decent society as one which does not corrupt the integrity of its people, we would have too narrow a definition. The definition would disqualify a society from being decent if it used even proper means to cause its criminals to abandon their integrity. But if by integrity we mean moral integrity, then the definition is too broad. A social order that violates the moral integrity of its dependents creates a humiliating society. Violation of moral integrity is sufficient for branding a society as humiliating, although it is not a necessary condition.

Dignity

Another suggestion to be considered is that a decent society is one whose institutions do not violate the dignity of the people in its orbit. The question is how this suggestion differs from the one suggesting that it is people's self-respect that must not be violated by the institutions of a decent society. What is the difference between dignity and self-respect?

Dignity is similar to pride. Pride is the expression of self-esteem; dignity is the expression of the feeling of respect persons feel toward themselves as human beings. Dignity constitutes the external aspect of self-respect. Self-respect is the attitude persons have to the fact of their being human. Dignity consists of the behavioral tendencies that attest to the fact that one's attitude toward oneself is an attitude of self-respect. Dignity is the tendency to behave in a dignified manner which attests to one's self-respect. One may have self-respect without possessing dignity. Self-respect is tested negatively; dignity is tested positively. This means that self-respect is typically revealed when a person's honor is violated, that is, when he is humiliated. His behavior at such a time is the sign of his self-respect. A person with dignity, in contrast, demonstrates her self-respect through positive acts which are not responses to provocations. In this way she signals that she will fight like a lioness if anyone tries to take away her self-respect.

In my discussion of the relation between humiliation and the violation of rights I emphasized that violating rights, especially human rights, can be a paradigmatic example of humiliation. But there is more to humiliation than the violation of rights. Humiliation is in part the result of humiliating gestures that are not naturally related to rights. What this adds is that humiliating gestures violate the dignity of the victim, while the violation of rights involves a diminution of self-respect. Dignity is the representation of self-respect.

If dignity is the external aspect of self-respect, why is it important? Perhaps paying attention to people's dignity means relating to the role-playing aspect of self-respect, to the masks they wear as self-respecting people. Wouldn't this mean returning to Aristotle's error? Aristotle, in his description of people possessing a "great soul" *(megalopsychia)*, claimed that honor and dishonor are the important issues. The "show" people put on for their neighbors ("A slow step is thought proper to the great-souled man, a deep voice and a level utterance . . ."; *Nichomachean Ethics* 1125 [Book IV, Chap. 3]) is considered mere "honor games"—that is, something not to be taken seriously. Aristotle would defend himself by saying that he was not giving stage directions for people who want to pretend that they have a great soul. He even goes into a detailed description of how ludicrous it is when people adorn themselves as if they had a great soul. He simply believed that he was describing the way a truly great-souled man actually behaves.

It might seem that the same is true of dignity. If dignity

is the behavioral expression of one's self-respect, then people who do not have this sense of self-respect can only pretend. However, dignity is not a presentation but a representation of self-respect.

One may still ask why people's dignity should be taken so seriously that wounding it is considered humiliating. An analogy with the concepts of honoring God and of holiness may be helpful. There is an internal relation between these two concepts. Holiness is the realm of the commandments and prohibitions concerned with honoring God. Violating these commandments is a desecration of holiness, which is a desecration of God's honor. God's honor dwells in the Temple and requires a special sort of behavior—holy rather than profane. Paul, in the New Testament, translates the idea of the Temple as the realm of holiness into the idea that the human body is a Temple, in that a divine spark dwells in every human being. Human honor is the honor of the Temple which serves as a dwelling place for the divine soul. This fact obliges people to be concerned that this Temple be a holy place worthy of housing God's honor. Violating the human body is violating the Temple, which means desecrating God's honor as well as human honor, since the latter is derived from the former. Analogously, human dignity is the behavior that sets the boundaries of human honor.

II

The Grounds of Respect

4

Justifying Respect

What aspect of human beings, if any, justifies respecting all human beings just because they are human? The "if any" in this question is not rhetorical. There is a serious possibility that there is no justification for respecting people solely because of their humanity, and that the most we can do is suggest a skeptical justification for respecting humans.

We will consider three types of justification: positive, skeptical, and negative. Positive justification means attempting to find a trait (or traits) belonging to all human beings, by virtue of which all people are worthy of basic respect. Skeptical justification means giving up the search for a justifying trait that is prior to the attitude of respect. Instead, the attitude of respect becomes the starting point, while the respect-evoking trait of being human is derived from this attitude itself. Negative justification means giving up the search for the trait in virtue of which human beings are deserving of respect and focusing instead on the question of why it is wrong to humiliate human beings.

This chapter deals with the positive justification of respect for human beings. Justification of such a kind is offered by the religions based on belief in creation and revelation. The answer they suggest to the question of why human beings are deserving of respect is that Man was created in God's image. The significance of this answer is that the respect every human being deserves is in virtue of reflected glory. It is not the human in people that justifies respect but the reflection of the divine, whether this is considered to be Man's soul, his external form, or anything else that can be included in the category of "God's image." Unqualified and unconditional honor (which in the case of God is called "glory") is merited only by God. Man is worthy only of reflected glory. This religious response is also meant to answer the question of why each person deserves the same attitude of respect. Each and every person was created in God's image. But what of the differences among people? Just as a mathematician dealing with infinite series can consider the differences among finite sections of these series as negligible, so anyone contemplating the differences among people in relation to the divinity must consider these differences negligible as well.

It is from the religious outlook that we get the idea of reflected glory as a basis of respect for human beings, but the idea of reflected glory is not limited to the reflection of the glory of God. Often we take pride in the achievements of "Man," which are not our own achievements at all: "Man" conquered the moon, "Man" discovered the method of immunization against polio, "Man" invented the airplane. These achievements were actually the achievements of individuals (even if, as in space flights, a large number of individuals were involved). The use of the sortal "Man" attests that the achievements of these individuals are considered the achievements of the entire human race, even though these individuals' achievements are not distributive. From the fact that Neil Armstrong landed on the moon it would indeed be lunatic on my part to argue that I too landed there. Yet the glory of that landing may be distributed and reflected among all human beings. The idea of reflected glory is meant to eliminate the question in virtue of what all people deserve respect. All that has to be done is to list "Man's achievements," add our belief that whoever has accomplished these wonderful things is surely deserving of honor, and then argue that the glory of these achievements emanates upon all members of the human race. If Buddha, Aristotle, Mozart, Shakespeare, and Newton constitute peaks of humanity, we participate in their glory even if we are only on the slopes.

But why should humans rather than songbirds deserve the reflected glory of Mozart's achievements? The common response is that humans and not songbirds are made in Mozart's image. Whoever is made in the same image deserves the glory—the reflected glory. Shakespeare is a source of pride for all of us. But what do "all of us" have in common? What is common to a Sumo wrestler, a Soho pimp, a Soweto salesperson, and me that gives Shakespeare the power to bestow reflected glory on all of us? Why shouldn't this reflected glory be bestowed on a narrower group, say the British, who "contributed" Shakespeare and Newton, but withheld from other groups, say the Albanians, who may not have contributed anyone with the power to confer glory on all other human beings?

This is only one problem with the idea of reflected

glory. Another difficulty may be illustrated by the following example. The record high jump for human beings is about eighteen inches above the jumper's own height, while a flea can jump a hundred times its own height. Why shouldn't we speak of flean glory in virtue of the flea who jumped so high and bestowed its glory on the other fleas? In light of the amazing jumping achievements of fleas, why shouldn't we provide them with training camps for jumping instead of trying to exterminate them?

We are faced with two complementary difficulties: (1) Why shouldn't reflected glory be confined to a narrower set than all human beings? (2) Why shouldn't it be extended to a larger set comprising other living creatures, such as fleas, who are capable of achievements so much greater than ours? Before we transfer the argument about reflected glory from God to fleas, I have one defensive argument for limiting reflected glory to the human race. The narrowest natural kind for being in Shakespeare's image is the human species, homo sapiens. The British do not constitute a natural kind, and so they cannot be the narrowest natural kind resembling the individual because of whom we are entitled to respect. At the same time, although the primates do constitute a natural kind, and even though the other primates do resemble human beings in various ways, they too do not satisfy the condition of being the narrowest natural kind. The human race is the narrowest natural kind for the relation of reflected glory.

But there is another aspect to the second claim. Even if human respect should be confined to the human race, how can we respond to the claim that each species deserves its own respect and there is no reason to single out respect for humans? The appropriate response here is that each species really does deserve its own respect and that respect for humans is not the same as, say, respect for panthers. If the glory of panthers is their fast running, then we can respect them by not confining them to restrictive cages.

All these defensive arguments may seem trivial, but they raise a serious issue: Why are natural kinds the appropriate categories for the moral question of who deserves human respect? A natural kind is a class that has explanatory power in the empirical realm and allows us to make many generalizations and predictions. But why is it appropriate for moral issues? If we were to find out that the group which bestows respect on others is the group of adult males, and that they constitute the narrowest natural kind, would we then restrict the group deserving of respect and deny it to women? Do we have to guarantee Mother Teresa a place in the pantheon of respect-bestowers in order for women to be included in the class of "God's image"? But even if we assume that the narrowest natural kind is homo sapiens, the question remains: Why are natural kinds relevant to the moral question of respect for humans? Such respect must be based on a trait that is morally relevant rather than on some "natural" achievement. Reflected glory based on a natural rather than a morally significant trait cannot be a reason for respecting people, even if it justifies granting them social honor.

As for respecting animals, this is clearly an anthropomorphic concept of respect. We do not grant any special respect to scallops and scorpions, not because they have no "achievements" but because we don't know how to "humanize" their achievements. (Cold-blooded animals seem less "human" to us.) The animals we feel obligated to honor are those that have become outstanding human symbols in our culture. Taking an eagle, which is a symbol of freedom or mastery, and restricting its ability to fly by putting it in a cage, is a violation of its essence and has a different meaning than caging a parrot. When we speak about respecting an animal we are really speaking about respecting ourselves. When we worry about respecting a chimp that is being mockingly mimicked by onlookers at the zoo, we are really worrying about respect for ourselves.

The move we have made in this section, which began with the religious response to the question of justifying human respect, is the move of reflected glory. This idea can take various and occasionally strange forms, in accordance with the beings that are supposed to confer their honor on their associates: God on Man, superior people on the rest of humanity, and finally humans on "humanoid" animals.

Traits Justifying Respect for Human Beings

Any trait that is a candidate for justifying the requirement of treating all human beings with respect must satisfy the following constraints:

1. The trait must not be graded, since respect must be given equally to all human beings.
2. The trait must not be of the sort that can be abused— namely, that can provide a reason for abhorrence or disrespect.

3. The trait must be morally relevant to respecting humans.
4. The trait must provide a humanistic justification for respect—that is, the justification must be made only in human terms, without appealing to divine entities.

Kant says he is grateful to Rousseau for teaching him how to respect human nature. This is not the gratitude of one zoologist to another for calling his attention to an interesting class of animals. Rousseau called Kant's attention to traits indicating the intrinsic worth people have just because they are human. Indeed, Kant divides the trait of humanity into the components that give it value:

1. Being a creature who determines ends, that is, a creature who gives things value.
2. Being a creature with the capacity for self-legislation.
3. Having the ability to perfect oneself—that is, to achieve greater and greater perfection.
4. Having the capacity to be a moral agent.
5. Being rational.
6. Being the only creature capable of transcending natural causality.[1]

This is not the entire list, but there is no doubt that the traits listed by Kant as the basis for justifying respect for humans fulfill the requirement of moral relevance (condition 3) and the humanistic requirement (condition 4). These traits do not, however, satisfy the first two conditions—that they should not be graded and that they should not be capable of being abused. The traits listed by Kant are possessed by different people in different degrees. One person's moral ability as a self-legislator is not the same as another's. The traits in Kant's list are ranking traits that do not justify what Kant wanted to justify: equal respect for all human beings just because they are human.

But more worrying than the fact that these traits can be ranked is the fact that they can be abused. If someone possesses the Kantian traits, such as the ability to lead a moral life, yet lives an obviously immoral life, why should that person be granted respect? On the contrary, the fact that the person is betraying his ability to lead a moral life is a reason to despise and even humiliate him as a desecrator of his appointed task rather than a reason to respect him. Criminals with the capacity to be moral, according to this view, are not worthy of respect, since they have desecrated their humanity—that is, the very nature that was supposed to serve as a source of respect for them. Similarly, we are not obligated to respect people who set evil goals for themselves, such as Nazi goals. People who fulfill their goals by sending other human beings to death camps should be degraded as fully as possible. The reason for respecting people as determiners of their own ends is also a reason for disrespecting them when they choose despicable ones. The ability to determine ends is not worthy of respect in and of itself. It is worthy of respect only when the ends are worthy ones. I consider respecting a trait to mean valuing the trait as a morally positive one. One may obviously also be impressed by the use of a human trait for evil—by the courage and daring of the gangster John Dillinger, for example—but in my terms being impressed does not mean feeling respect. Marlow, the marvelous narrator created by Joseph Conrad, is deeply impressed by Kurtz's hypnotic demons, but he certainly does not feel moral respect for them.

Anyone who justifies respecting humans in the spirit of Kant's list of traits has a clear line of defense against the criticism that, since these traits are graded, they cannot justify equal respect for everyone. The line of defense is that, even if a trait is graded, one can still hold that there is a threshold for its existence in people, a limit that guarantees basic respect for all human beings. Anything above this threshold is a basis for social evaluation according to the degree and strength of the trait in any particular individual. This limit guarantees the basic respect all humans are equally entitled to, while anything above the limit is not egalitarian, and rightfully so. Consider, for example, the trait of rationality. We can determine that the threshold that justifies respecting humans as opposed to animals is their ability to act for a reason. This threshold guarantees respect for every person capable of acting on the basis of reasons. The quality of these reasons may be ranked to provide a basis for the graded evaluation of people, but this ranking must be separated from the issue of basic human respect.

This move is a good one if the trait justifying respect exists to a positive degree in everyone and the problem is only securing enough of it for each person. But, as mentioned, the Kantian traits also have the capacity to be abused, so that the existence of the ability is not a guarantee against negative evaluation.

The Kantian traits do not exhaust all the possible suggestions for traits that might justify respecting humans. Thus, for example, Bernard Williams offers the interesting suggestion that every human being has his own point of view that cannot be replaced by anyone else's and thus has unique value.[2] An obvious question is why a point of view is more precious, and of greater moral relevance, than a fingerprint, which is also unique to each person. But even if we presume that an answer to the question can be found, we would still remain with the question of whether there might not be negative points of view. What is there in Iago's evil point of view that makes it worthy of basic respect? Why isn't Iago's point of view a justification for insulting him, since it is such a malicious one? Even if we admit that Iago's point of view has a great deal to teach us about human nature, its instructive value is purely instrumental and does not provide intrinsic value. Not everything we can learn from has intrinsic value. After all, even if Josef Mengele's monstrous twin experiments had been able to teach us something about human endurance, this would not lessen their enormity. Information from evil sources, though possibly instructive, cannot have intrinsic value. Even if we think that Iago's or Richard III's point of view is worthy of preservation, this does not mean that we justify preserving it because of some basic respect.

Another problem is that the idea of a unique viewpoint justifying basic respect fails to fulfill the moral relevance condition. Having a large number of points of view is humanly important as a source of variety in human experience, which can teach us about human nature. It is therefore perhaps more important to sustain a variety of points of view than to maintain different observation posts on the stars and the far-flung galaxies, but this does not imply that the bearers of these points of view deserve any more respect than the powerful telescopes through which we investigate the stars.

The Intrinsic Value Constraint

We are still searching for traits justifying respect for humans. Kant adds an additional constraint on the choice of such traits—namely, that the traits should justify granting every human being intrinsic value. But what is the intrinsic value that is supposed to be justified by the traits?

The distinction between use value and exchange value goes back at least to Adam Smith. Use value is the value of the benefit obtained from an object in the fulfillment of human ends. Exchange value is the object's power to induce other people to give up other objects of value in order to obtain it. Another name for exchange value is price. The idea behind the distinction between use value and price is that use value does not depend solely or even primarily on people's subjective evaluation of the object, but rather on its objective contribution to the achievement of human ends. Even if the exchange value of diamonds, for example, is very high due to their rarity, their use value is much lower.

An object's exchange value, as the name suggests, is based on the idea that the object in question is considered replaceable. But use value as well is based on the possibility of substitution, since an object's use value is the value it has as a tool for the advancement of human ends. Tools can always be replaced. Sometimes the replacement may be less efficient in achieving the desired end, but replacement remains possible.

Intrinsic value, in contrast, is based on the idea that the

valuable object is irreplaceable. God may be able to compensate Job for the loss of his property in the horrendous
trial he underwent by giving him new property, but when
He grants Job a number of children double that of the
number of his children who died, this cannot constitute a
compensation or replacement. Job's children had an intrinsic value that even God cannot replace by providing
him with new ones.

Kant's central claim is that every person has intrinsic
value. This claim does not imply that there can be no
situation in which it is acceptable to judge people in terms
of replacement, but only that there are some contexts in
which it is unacceptable to do so. Thus, according to Kant,
the main constraint on traits that justify granting people
respect is that the traits must also justify granting human
beings intrinsic value—not use value and certainly not
exchange value.

The various well-known forms of utilitarianism do not
accept this. They deny that the traits that make people
worthy of respect in virtue of their humanity must also
be traits that justify the stipulation that there are situations
in which people are irreplaceable. Utilitarianism denies
that this requirement is constitutive of respect for humans. According to this view, the concept of intrinsic value
has no moral application and is nothing but a rhetorical
device for saying that something is very important to us
and is therefore irreplaceable. All that irreplaceability
means is that under normal circumstances we will refuse
to bargain about the thing that is so important to us. But
for every terrible human situation, there is an even worse
situation whose prevention justifies choosing the lesser
evil, even if this choice is as monstrous as Sophie's choice

(in William Styron's novel). Avoiding choice in such a situation is moral cowardice, says the utilitarian, not a manifestation of acknowledging people's "intrinsic value." The intrinsic value justification is exclusionary. It claims that under certain circumstances in which it is necessary to discuss replacement of people one may not enter into pro and con arguments, since those whose fate is being decided have an intrinsic value that cannot be given a price tag and that cannot be assessed in terms of the substitution of one for another, even if the "other" includes many people in exchange for one.

Do Kant's justifying traits actually abide by the intrinsic-value constraint? Take the trait of rationality, for instance: in its "purest" manifestation, in angels, all individuality vanishes. It is no tragedy if Gabriel is replaced by Michael. This intuition can be formulated in Aristotelian terms: Man's individuality is determined by the matter that distinguishes one person from another, while people's rational form may be shared by many of them. Thus human rationality permits the replacement of one person by another sharing the same (rational) form. In this sense Williams's uniqueness of point of view is a trait that fits the irreplaceability requirement better than the Kantian traits.

In my list of constraints on traits justifying respect for humans I do not include the Kantian constraint of intrinsic value—the claim that only traits which confer intrinsic value can justify respecting people as human, while traits with instrumental value cannot be justifying traits of this sort. If we add this requirement on justifying traits, then the irreplaceability constraint will severely restrict the search for such traits.

Radical Freedom as a Justifying Trait

We continue, then, our search for a human trait or traits that can justify respecting people. We have not yet distinguished between capacity traits and achievement traits. A capacity trait is the human potential to achieve a desired end; an achievement trait is one in which a human capacity is put to use. Both capacity traits and achievement traits can be ranking traits. Achievements are not distributed evenly among people, and the distribution of capacities among people is not equal either.

The trait I would like to suggest for justifying respect for humans is based on a capacity. The capacity is that of reevaluating one's life at any given moment, as well as the ability to change one's life from this moment on.

What is involved here is the ability of human beings to repent of their sins, in the secular sense of this concept—that is, to abandon their evil ways. The claim is that humans have this ability. Even if there are noticeable differences among people in their ability to change, they are deserving of respect for the very possibility of changing. Even the worst criminals are worthy of basic human respect because of the possibility that they may radically reevaluate their past lives and, if they are given the opportunity, may live the rest of their lives in a worthy manner. We are not talking here about the honor people deserve for their achievements. Granting respect on the basis of the possibility of change is oriented toward what people can do in the future rather than what they have done in the past. People deserve respect not for the degree of power they have to change their way of life in the future, but for the very possibility that they may be able to change. Thus respecting humans means never giving up on anyone, since all people are capable of living dramatically differently from the way they have lived so far.

Kant does indeed speak of Man as worthy of respect because he is free from the causal web of Nature, but Kant was not talking about "empirical Man." The present claim, however, is that a person who is really radically free is worthy of respect. Radical freedom means that, although a person's past actions, character, and environment constitute a set of constraints on her future actions, they nevertheless do not determine these actions. Every person is capable of a future way of life that is discontinuous with the past. The respect people deserve for this is based precisely on the fact that Man does not have a nature, if a "nature" means a set of character traits that determine one's actions. Animals have natures, human beings do not.

There is a deep analogy between the concept of linguistic meaning and the concept of the meaning of life. Linguistic meaning accords with the possibility that the series of uses a term has had in the past does not determine its uses in the future. Linguistic uses are not railroad tracks set up in advance, so that the only thing to worry about is the possibility of the engine going off the track. The same is true of the meaning of life: not only do the totality of all one's past actions fail to determine the path of one's future actions, but even the interpretation one has given to one's past actions can be reevaluated at any given moment. The engine of life can change direction at the will of the driver, even if some directions are easier to travel in than others.

What should we say about an evil person who has been given an opportunity to contemplate his life but who validates his evil life out of his own free choice? Does this amount to a violation of our second criterion, that the trait justifying respect should not be capable of being abused? Nicolae Ceauşescu believed that he was acting like a patriot developing his country. Is there any value to the fact that he was free to choose? Eichmann, after his trial in Jerusalem, confirmed his life as a Nazi out of his own choice. Shouldn't the *content* of one's choice be the source of respect, not the mere possibility of choice? The two evildoers I have mentioned, Ceauşescu and Eichmann, lived and died as villains. Their end did not atone for their lives. But the respect I am talking about is not, as I have stressed, respect for past achievements, and it is not anchored in the degree of one's ability to change in the future. The source of this respect is the fact that the future remains open. Respecting people preserves the idea that their future is open, and that they can change their lives for the better through action or a reevaluation of their past.

The problem with this suggestion for justifying respect for humans through radical freedom obviously lies in the question of whether human beings really are free in a radical sense. B. F. Skinner rightly connects the concept of dignity with the concept of freedom, except that in his view the concept of freedom required for the concept of dignity is indefensible. In his opinion the difference between freedom and lack of freedom is the difference between covert and overt conditioning. In the former case it is more difficult for outside observers to see the connection between the stimulus and the response, but in both cases human responses are controlled by conditioning. The sense of dignity as liberation from control by stimuli is in Skinner's view an illusion. The most one can aim for is to replace negative, aversive stimuli by overt positive ones. This is the sole difference between the dystopia of *1984* and the utopia of *Walden II*.

Dignity is, in Skinner's opinion, an illusory idea, and so it is risky to base social theories on it. Instead, the desired society must be based on positive conditioning. The difference between a free person and a slave is in the nature of the stimuli activating them: the former enjoys rewarding stimuli; the latter suffers from punishing ones. The "rebirth" of a person who has lived a life of sin is not the result of a free act of choice but the result of conditioning. In principle Albert Speer repenting of his misdeeds is no different from Alex in "A Clockwork Orange" undergoing brutal conditioning with sophisticated equipment. The difference between them lies in the fact that in the case of Speer we cannot see the stimuli overtly, as we can in the case of Alex. But this is the only difference. The possibility of radical change in one's future conduct is the result of conditioning and not of choice. It thus cannot serve as a justification for human dignity.

The trait I am suggesting as the justification for granting respect to every person as a human being—the ability in principle to change one's life—depends upon the answer to the question of whether human beings actually have this ability. But one could say that the entire quest for a justification for respecting humans assumes that they do, since the sort of justification that involves praise and blame assumes that people can act otherwise. Thus if I am mistaken in assuming that people possess the freedom necessary to justify respect, my error involves not only the choice of the justifying trait but also the very possibility of justifying anything at all in the moral domain.

There is a more serious criticism of the justification for

respecting humans on the basis of their ability to repent. It is that this justification does not satisfy the requirement that respect must not be accorded for a capacity that could be used for evil. But if the justifying trait is the capacity for radically changing one's life in the process of repentance—that is, the human ability to act freely—then this is a capacity that can work both ways: not only to change from bad to good but also to change from good to bad. Tolstoy's Father Sergei exemplifies the possibility of changing in both directions within one lifetime. Focusing on one direction, the ability to change for the good, is a blunder made by all those who have tried to find a trait that justifies respect for humans and ignored its potential bad effects.

There is a great deal of truth in this criticism of the capacity to repent as the trait justifying respect for human beings. Yet there is also something in this trait that makes it different from the other Kantian traits, including the one of fitness for a moral life. The capacity for repentance addresses itself directly to a context in which the issue of human respect arises most sharply—that is, the case in which human beings live a life of evil. The question in this case is why even the wicked deserve respect.

Consider first the easy case of someone who has lived a moral life and can clearly be respected for this. It would then be strange to cease respecting her only because she has the capacity to stop living a moral life and to adopt an evil mode of existence instead. Someone who is living a moral life deserves respect for a proven achievement rather than a potential capacity. A person's achievement in leading a moral life creates the presumption in her favor that she will continue living this way, unless the opposite is shown to be true. Such a presumption is acquired by actually living a moral life. It is not a presumption existing from birth, as is the Kantian trait of the capacity for a moral life, but rather one acquired through effort.

Now what about the evildoer who lives a wicked life, and who is very likely to continue in this wretched existence? Likelihood must not be confused with presumption. Even though it is likely that she will continue living this way, this likelihood should not be turned into a presumption, because in principle an evildoer has the capacity to change and repent. This capacity implies that she deserves basic respect as a human being who should not be "given up on," precisely because there is a chance, no matter how small, that she will repent.

Thus in one direction the human capacity for living a moral life deserves respect in that it is a proven ability that constitutes a presumption for the future, while in the other direction respect should be based on the presumption that human beings are capable of changing their life.

5

The Skeptical Solution

The skeptical solution to the problem of finding a trait that could justify respecting people as human beings reflects skepticism about the existence of such a trait. The skeptical solution is not a nihilistic one. Nihilistic solutions claim that the absence of traits justifying respect implies that people should not be respected because they do not have any value. The skeptical solution, in contrast, is based on the fact that in our way of life people believe that human beings deserve respect. Skeptics see this fact, rather than any particular human trait, as the final justification for respecting people as human beings. In the skeptical solution the attitude of respect toward people has priority over any possible human trait due to which they may deserve this respect.

An analogy may be helpful here. Old, outdated economic theories attempted to explain the puzzling fact that people are willing to exchange desirable and useful goods and services for pieces of paper (known as money) whose value as paper does not justify giving up anything for them. The explanation for this common but odd practice used to be the argument that paper money has value because it is backed by gold: at any time one can demand gold in exchange for a bill. Paper money is nothing but a promissory note from its producer to exchange it for gold on demand. This theory is indeed based on historical fact, but the value of money is not an effect of the backing that the money actually has; it is rather a result of the fact that people are willing to accept it. Thus the value money has is that given it by people: it is not based on any property of money in and of itself apart from people's willingness to accept it.

Human value, according to the skeptical solution, is acquired similarly. Human beings have value because others value them, and not because of any prior characteristic that justifies such valuing. Because our form of life actually does assign value to human beings, the result is that the characteristic of being human, which is supposed to justify respect, is actually parasitic on the attitude of valuing humans. The skeptical solution turns the relation of justification on its head: it is not some human trait that justifies the attitude of respect for people as human beings, but the attitude of respect for human beings that gives value to the trait of being human.

An immediate criticism of the skeptical move says that if "our" form of life actually does include a basic attitude of respect for people as human beings, this is a remnant of the religious view that sees humans as created in God's image. The religious view grants respect to all human beings as descendants of Adam. But even if this claim is a correct description of how the attitude of respecting humans came into being in societies that were influenced by the revealed religions, this does not mean that the claim of "creation in God's image" is our justification for respecting people today. Undoubtedly one of the reasons people are willing to accept paper money is the historical fact that in the past these bills constituted promissory notes for which the bearer could obtain an appropriate quantity of gold on demand. Many people continued to believe that paper money still possessed this feature even after most economies had abandoned the gold standard. But even if these facts provide a historical explanation for people's willingness to honor paper money, they cannot justify the current value of these bills, since their value is presently based solely on people's willingness to accept them and not on anything else. Analogously, the context in which respect for humans emerged is not the context in which it maintains its justification.

Another, more pointed criticism is that if "our" form of life is indeed one in which respect for humans is safeguarded, then all societies based on our form of life rule out humiliation, and so by definition they are all decent. It is therefore unnecessary to delve into the issue of the source of respect for humans in order to anchor a decent society in it, since such societies already exist. The need for justification arises only when there is some problem. If the decent society already exists, almost by default, then there is no need to justify anything. The reason we do feel this need is that many, if not all, societies are not decent and trample on human dignity—even societies that have claimed to share our form of life. Since this is the case, it is impossible to anchor respect in an attitude that is supposed to exist in our form of life—a supposed attitude of safeguarding respect for humans.

Either way, according to this criticism, there is no need to justify respect for humans. If the skeptical solution holds, then there is no need for justification because the solution secures the sort of decent society that does not require justification. But if the skeptical solution does not hold, because people are not in fact respected as humans, then the proposed justification is useless, since it is empty even as a skeptical justification. Either way, it is pointless.

The way to resolve the last criticism is connected with the distinction between the act of treating people with respect and the notion of respect itself. A society may be humiliating in its concrete treatment of those dependent on it, while still having a clear concept of the respect that should be granted to all people as human beings. Such societies' hypocrisy, which inheres in the gap between what they say and what they do concerning human dignity, is good evidence that they are aware of the concept of human dignity and the need to respect it. What is needed for the skeptical solution to the problem of justifying respect for humans is not the strong requirement of actually treating people with respect but only the general idea of respect—that is, a principled position or approach of this sort. Moreover, a society in which there is intentional humiliation—on the part of institutions or individuals—is grounded in the assumption that both the humiliator and the victim share a concept of human dignity; otherwise there is no point in the act of humiliation.

An additional disturbing criticism of the skeptical solution demands a separate discussion. This is the argument that the justification of respect on the basis of an existing attitude, without the need for reasons, could just as easily serve as a justification for a racist attitude that grants respect only to the members of a "superior" race and humiliates the members of "inferior" races.

The Skeptical Solution as a Racist Solution

According to the skeptical solution, the justification for respecting people as having value is the fact that we have an attitude of respect for all humans. Had the facts been such that this attitude of respect were limited and not directed at all human beings—if, for example, the Greeks respected only the Greeks and not the barbarians, the Jews respected only the Jews and not the Gentiles, the Germans respected only the Aryans and not the Jews, the whites respected only the whites and not the blacks—then each such community would have a skeptical justification for respecting only its own members and not strangers. The strangers would not be worthy of respect simply by virtue of the fact that they were not respected. This argument raises two problems: (1) Why should all people be respected, rather than only some of them? (2) Why should we stop at humans and not accord other living beings, such as fleas, the same respect we accord humans?

When considering the racist solution—the solution attributing "human dignity" only to some human beings and not to all of them—it is important to distinguish between trait-racism and attitude-racism. Trait-racism is the view that ascribes to members of one's own race (in the broad sense of the term) some trait such that only creatures possessing that trait are worthy of basic respect as human beings, while those who lack it are considered subhuman and unworthy of such respect. In general, trait-racists do not constitute a problem for the skeptical justification of human dignity, because the trait they ascribe to members of their own race and deny to other people either is based on an empirically false racist theory or lacks moral relevance. Thus trait-racism is not skeptical racism.

A hard case presented by the trait-racist—and one that is not necessarily based on an empirical error—is the case of retarded persons. In this case the trait-racist's error is moral rather than empirical. But the case of the retarded seems to me to constitute a serious reason not to base the attitude of respect for humans on a Kantian justifying trait such as rationality, moral capacity, or the like. This case also provides an important argument in favor of the skeptical justification.

Trait-racists often begin with the retarded and move on to members of other races. The "final solution" for the Jews and the Gypsies was preceded by the "euthanasia campaign" in which the retarded were the first to be murdered in gas chambers. The methods used in the extermination camps were first developed for exterminating the retarded.

Attitude-racism is not, as far as I know, a position that has actually been held by any group, but it is a conceptually possible position. The attitude-racist says, "I cannot explain why only the members of my group are worthy of the respect that you universalists believe all people deserve for some reason, but it is a fact that my group has an attitude of respect only toward members of the group, while our attitude toward the other creatures that are called human is not different from your own attitude to pets. And since it is a fact that this is our attitude, it constitutes a skeptical justification for respecting only the members of our group and not others. Anyone who isn't one of us is valueless because we don't ascribe value to them. I don't see how your inflationary attitude of attributing 'human value' to all people has any advantage over the deflationary attitude of our form of life, which limits respect to the members of our own group." The attitude-racist might add that even though the familiar form of racism is trait-racism, this is really just an unsuccessful rationalization—an attempt to anchor the racist attitude in a so-called objective trait. Honest racists could justify their racism—although obviously not under that pejorative label—with the claim that their limited attitude of respect is the attitude that exists in their form of life. This attitude constitutes the justification for limiting respect to the members of their group.

One way to argue against racism is to claim that, since all the existing types are trait-racism, it follows that even racist theory has a presumption in favor of human dignity as the dignity all people are entitled to. Racists try to reject this presumption with feeble excuses about supposed flaws in members of other races in order to deny them human dignity. But since trait-racism is the only form of racism that actually exists, we may ignore attitude-racism in practice; its importance is purely conceptual. At the same time, attitude-racism presents a real problem for the skeptical justification for respecting every human being as human. The conceptual problem posed by attitude-racism cannot be brushed aside with the argument that historically no one has ever justified racism this way.

The skeptical justification of respect for humans, which despairs of finding a relevant trait justifying the granting of respect to all human beings and makes do with the fact that respecting people is part of our form of life, has a complementary aspect: respecting people regardless of what group they may belong to is the attitude that best fits our moral judgments. In other words, we feel that justification based on an existent attitude of respect is also the best justification when considerations of coherence are taken into account. A racist attitude, which restricts human dignity to a subgroup of human beings, is not coherent with the rest of our moral judgments. The first person plural in the expression "our moral judgments" includes everyone who belongs to our form of life. I am speaking not of coherence with some moral theory, but of coherence with the judgments of our form of life. These judgments are not necessarily all coherent with one another, but the assumption that all humans are worthy of respect brings them together better than any alternative.

The justification in terms of coherence applies not only against the racist view but also against the idea of extending the attitude of respect due to human beings so as to include all living creatures. We can envisage a different form of life whose attitude toward animals is different from ours—for example, the attitude expressed in Walt Whitman's portrayal:

> They do not sweat and whine about their condition;
> They do not lie awake in the dark and weep for their sins;
> They do not make me sick discussing their duty to God;
> Not one is dissatisfied—not one is demented with the mania of owning things;
> Not one kneels to another, nor to his kind that lived thousands of years ago.[1]

But even if we do not see animals as possessing the superlative traits Whitman ascribes to them—with not a little criticism of us humans—we can still see how a form of life different from our own could be included in the circle of respect for living creatures, whether all or some of them. The question then is why stop at human beings in granting basic respect. Here too the skeptical answer must be that the restriction of respect to human beings is justified because it coheres better with the totality of moral judgments in our form of life than extending this attitude to living creatures in general. This does not deny the urgent need to improve our attitude toward animals; however, the problem in this attitude is not humiliation but cruelty, and the solution is considering the animals' pain. In our form of life, in contrast, a major problem in our relations toward other people is humiliation, and the solution is respect. We must take a stance of "respect and suspect" toward societies with forms of life that differ from ours, which preach about extending the attitude of respect to all living creatures. These societies do not always have an outstanding record of respecting human beings.

A Negative Justification of Human Dignity

Justifying human dignity negatively means not aspiring to provide a justification for respecting people, but only for not humiliating them. In a certain sense this is all we need for explicating the concept of a decent society, since it has been defined negatively, as a nonhumiliating society, rather than positively, as a society that safeguards human dignity.

A negative justification is not a skeptical justification. Rather, it is based on the fact that human beings are creatures capable of feeling pain and suffering not only as a result of physically painful acts but also as a result of acts with symbolic meaning. Man, in the words of Ernst Cassirer, is a symbolic animal—that is, an animal that lives in symbols. The human capacity for symbol-based anguish in addition to physical suffering constitutes a trait that justifies nonhumiliation. The argument as a whole is as follows. Cruelty is the ultimate evil. Preventing cruelty is the supreme moral commandment. Humiliation is the extension of cruelty from the physical to the psychological realm of suffering. Humiliation is mental cruelty. A decent society must be committed not only to the eradication of physical cruelty in its institutions but also to the elimination of mental cruelty caused by these institutions.

The capacity to tolerate mental cruelty, like the capacity to bear physical pain, is not evenly distributed among human beings. Some people are highly sensitive to humiliation, and their entire spiritual being is shaken in the face of its manifestations. Others may be immune to such manifestations, either because they are equipped with the hide of an elephant or because they have such a well-developed mechanism of self-deception that they can see spit as rain. Doesn't this make the justifying trait for nonhumiliation a graded trait, and the attitude to the potential victims of humiliation a graded attitude, in proportion to their sensitivity to pain and insult?

This last question relates to our constraints on the traits that can justify respecting humans, which include the requirement that the justifying trait should not justify gradations of respect. But these constraints do not apply to the negative justification, because the justification for the requirement of nonhumiliation comes from the need to avoid cruelty, humiliation being considered an aspect of cruelty. It is essential not to treat people cruelly, and the issue of equality does not arise. What is necessary is nonhumiliation, and equal nonhumiliation. The issue of ranking people's capacity to suffer simply does not arise in the negative justification.

One possible criticism of the above analysis is this. The argument that humiliation is wrong because it is mental cruelty, and that the evil in cruelty requires no demonstration, is an argument which suffers from a familiar sort of category mistake. The expression "mental cruelty" belongs to a family of expressions including "spiritual extermination" and "mental illness." All of them assume that the noun denotes something with two aspects. There is physical extermination and spiritual extermination. There is physical illness and mental illness. Analogously, there is physical cruelty and there is also mental cruelty: one is based on physical pain, and the other on psychological pain. When Golda Meir spoke about the assimilation of Jews as "spiritual extermination"—which she considered even worse than physical extermination in gas chambers—and when people are incarcerated in a mental hospital because they are "mentally ill," the same sort of mistake is being made. It is assumed that there is an expression here that consists of a noun and an adjective, and that it behaves like the expressions "round table" and "rectangular table." But just as the expression "round-table" has the idiomatic usage of "discussion by equals," and in this usage is not a combination of "round" and "table," so the expression "spiritual extermination" is not extermination from a spiritual point of view and "mental illness" is not illness from a mental point of view. Critics might claim that this is true of "mental cruelty" as well. Humiliation is humiliation, and it is bad enough, but it is not similar to and does not constitute physical abuse by different means. An epigram by the seventeenth-century letter-writer Marie de Sévigné expresses it this way: "There is no real ill in life except severe bodily pain; everything else is the child of imagination." This should serve as a warning signal, say the critics. Physical cruelty is indeed the mother of all evil, and next to it humiliation is an ordinary vice.

My response to this criticism is that the sort of mental cruelty manifested in humiliation is cruelty in a very literal sense. Very often a humiliating act is accompanied by a physically painful act in such a way that injury is added to insult. Marie de Sévigné's epigram undoubtedly contains a kernel of truth, but its shell is misleading. The kernel of truth is that in the short run, which is generally the range of physical pain, most people prefer to be rid of it at any price, including the price of humiliation. But this does not mean that it is also people's clear preference in the long run. The psychological scars left by humiliation heal with greater difficulty than the physical scars of someone who has suffered only physical pain. The critic may reply that this is simply another instance of the metaphorical fallacy: "scars of humiliation" are not scars, and "psychic pain" is not pain. Humiliation is not cruelty if the connection is supposed to be one of meaning. But I continue to respond that humiliation is not restricted to symbolic acts, and may be accompanied by the production of physical pain. Psychological abuse is part of the meaning of cruelty, and therefore the supreme commandment of eradicating all manifestations of cruelty includes the eradication of humiliation. The continuum between physical cruelty and humiliation is illustrated by a newspaper article ("Humiliated into the Dirt," *Ha'aretz*, December 29, 1991) which discusses the humiliation of recruits at an army base:

> Sergeant Manny Mor ordered Private Ya'akov Yehezkel to swallow more and more water. When the poor private began vomiting, the sergeant forced him to continue drinking and ran to call the rest of the group to come and mimic their friend's vomiting. Toughening. Corporal Yosef Gohejan, for his part, kicked sand into the faces of privates lying on the ground, and forced a private with an injured hand to use that hand to lift a heavy object: more toughening. And both of them, Mor and Gohejan, made fun of another private, who stuttered: they mimicked him publicly.

The negative, indirect justification for human dignity, which justifies nonhumiliation, is based on the idea that any sort of cruelty toward man or beast is wrong. But only people suffer from the sort of cruelty that is humiliation—for example, having one's stammer mimicked—and a decent society is one that eradicates abuse, where humiliation is a particular form of abuse. The requirement of eradicating all cruelty, including humiliation, does not require any moral justification in its turn, since the paradigm example of moral behavior is behavior that prevents cruelty. This is where justification comes to an end.

6

Being Beastly to Humans

The expression "treating human beings as human," which occurs repeatedly in this book, is quite old, but that does not make it clear. Clarifying it is an important part of the attempt to explicate the concept of humiliation, since often to humiliate someone is to treat a human being as nonhuman. But what does it mean to treat a human as nonhuman? Is this actually possible?

The way to clarify this problem is by the method of contrast. That is, we must clarify what ways of treating humans stand in contrast with ways of treating them as nonhuman that have the potential for being humiliating. The last qualification is intended to exclude cases of treating humans as nonhuman which are not humiliating—for instance, treating them as gods or angels.

There are various ways of treating humans as nonhuman: (a) treating them as objects; (b) treating them as machines; (c) treating them as animals; (d) treating them as subhuman (which includes treating adults as children).

There is another, historically important, way of rejecting humans from the human commonwealth—treating individuals or groups of people as demons spreading absolute evil and destroying humanity. The witch craze that engulfed Europe in the sixteenth and seventeenth centuries is a literal manifestation of demonization—that is, associating unfortunate people, generally women, with the devil's realm. The demonization of the Jews by the Nazis is not literally associated with the realm of the devil, but the Nazis attributed nonhuman traits of evil and the desire for destruction to the Jewish "race."

What is bad about demonization is the aspect of evil. Deification—transforming a human into a god (as in the case of the Pharaohs)—is also a way of removing the person from the human commonwealth. But deification is the attribution of noble superhuman traits to a person; demonization is the attribution of evil superhuman traits. Demonization involves a tension between the two senses of humiliation—that of rejection from the human commonwealth and that of the loss of control. Demonization includes the first but not the second. On the contrary, it is often accompanied by a theory of a world conspiracy.

Societies often demonize external enemies rather than their own members or those directly subject to them. I have restricted my discussion to the issue of whether or not a society humiliates those subject to its authority. I do not discuss the question of whether a decent society must also refrain from humiliating its external enemies (for example, in its war propaganda). Therefore, according to my definition, a decent society may not use its institutions to demonize those who are dependent on it. And I am also willing to add without any additional argumentation that a decent society must restrict its humiliation of external enemies—for example, it must not dehumanize them through demonization.

We must distinguish between treating humans *as if* they were objects and treating them *as* objects. In the first case the "objectifier" does not actually believe that the people involved are things but simply treats them that way. In the second case the "objectifier" actually believes that the person toward whom the "thingish" behavior is directed is a sort of object. Analogous distinctions must be made between treating human beings *as if* they were machines and treating them *as* machines, or treating humans *as if* they were animals and treating them *as* animals.

Human beings are obviously also objects and animals, and even machines, but they are not merely objects or merely animals, and they are certainly not merely machines. "Treating humans as objects" means treating them merely as objects, and similarly for the other categories.

One claim might be that humans can treat others as if they were objects, as if they were machines, as if they were animals, but they cannot—except in pathological cases—actually treat them *as* objects, *as* machines, or even *as* animals. The sense in which humans cannot treat others as objects is like the sense in which humans in normal circumstances cannot look at a monkey and see it as a monkey wrench. This is not exactly a claim about a conceptual impossibility, but it is not simply a factual inability either.

This claim must be refined by another distinction, that between long-term and short-term treatment of human beings. In a rush to catch the train we may not notice if we are buying our ticket from a human like ourselves or a ticket-selling machine. But even in such circumstances we will be embarrassed if we realize that we have thanked an automatic machine. Even if we extend the short term from the time it takes to buy a ticket to the time it takes to perform a surgical operation, we are likely to discover behavior that might without difficulty be described literally as treating a human being as a machine. A surgeon may well treat the patient on the operating table as a (biological) machine. Doctors at their best concentrate through the monitor on the functional aspects of the human body in very much the same way that engineers at a space control center treat missiles when they malfunction. But even in cases like these we expect the surgeon to treat the anesthetized patient on the operating table differently from the way a veterinarian might treat a cow being operated on, and we expect both of them to have a different attitude than that of a mechanic working on a missile. This difference might be expressed, for example, if the operation goes wrong.

At any rate, the first step in our discussion involves the possibility of seeing humans in the long run literally as objects or machines. We have already denied this possibility, except when there is pathology in the observer, as may perhaps be the case in autism, or when there is pathology in the person being observed, as in the case of a "vegetable" who has irreparably lost consciousness and cognitive functioning and is being kept alive artificially by medical equipment. The unfortunate case of the "vegetable" may perhaps allow us to see the body attached to the equipment as an inanimate object rather than a human being, even for a long spell. And perhaps this is true *only* when a long spell is involved, as at first when the patient is in a coma those around her look for any possible glimmer of humanity. Only later does an objectifying view of the situation take over.

These pathological cases may help us understand what it means to be blind to the human aspect of persons. What I mean by blindness to the human aspect in people's long-term attitude toward other human beings is close to the literal meaning of color-blindness. If someone proclaims a nonracist attitude by claiming to be color-blind, she does not mean that she is literally unable to distinguish between black and white, but only that her human attitude toward black people and white people is not affected by the color of their skin. What I am talking about, however, is literal perception, and the question is what it means to be unable to perceive the human aspect in a human being.

A prior question is what it means to be able to see the human aspect in a human being. More precisely, what does it mean to see human beings as human in a long-range aspect? That is, how do we see humans? After discussing this question we will be able to clarify the issue of how we treat humans. The answers to the these questions are internally related to one another.

Seeing Humans

A painting of Picasso's from his Blue Period is literally blue. It is also a sad painting. It is not necessarily a painting that makes us sad, and the linen canvas on which it is painted is certainly incapable of feeling sadness. The painting expresses sadness. A painting can express sadness if it nonliterally exemplifies the label "sadness." A painting is not something that can feel emotions, and so it cannot be literally sad, but it can be sad in a nonliteral sense. Nelson Goodman, who originated this distinction, would say that the expression of sadness in the painting is a metaphorical exemplification of the linguistic term "sadness."[1] I hesitate to use the term "metaphor" here, and so I am using the generic term "nonliteral." My hesitation results from a controversy: it is sometimes said that a necessary condition for metaphor is that it can in principle be paraphrased, but when we say that a painting of Picasso's is sad there doesn't seem to be any other way of saying this.

A sad painting is also not necessarily a painting that makes us sad. We do not need to be sad in order to see and understand that the painting is a sad one. The painting of Picasso's is neither literally nor metaphorically sad, but it is sad in a nonliteral sense. In Wittgenstein's terminology, the picture is sad in a secondary sense.[2] A secondary sense of an expression is one that is not literal, yet cannot be paraphrased.

Mikhail Gorbachev's sad face at his farewell address was not literally sad. It was Gorbachev who was sad, literally—not his face. Seeing Gorbachev's face as sad means seeing it as expressing sadness. Seeing a human being as human means seeing the body as expressing the soul, as Wittgenstein put it. In other words, it means seeing the human body and its parts in the mental terms they nonliterally exemplify (in either a secondary or a metaphorical sense). We see persons as human when we see their expressions in human terms: this person has a friendly or a thoughtful face, a worried or a happy expression. When we see a human face we do not first notice that the lips are curved downward, that the eyebrows are lowered, that the head is sunk down on the chest, and that the cheeks have a gray texture—and then ask ourselves how to interpret this face. We see the face as sad just as we see the lips as curved downward: not as a result of hypothesis testing and deduction from evidence, but directly. Interpretation is a voluntary matter, but what we see is not voluntary. I see the sadness of Gorbachev's face just as I see the red birthmark on his forehead. I do not see either of them as the result of any decision on my part to see them that way. I see human beings in their human aspect not as an act of choice or decision, but because I cannot see otherwise. I can obviously be mistaken in what I see, whether I am seeing something under a physical (literal) label or under a psychological label (in a secondary sense). For example, Gorbachev's birthmark may be not red but blue-black, and his face may be not sad but despairing. The possibility of error, however, does not make my seeing a conjecture.

The general idea should be quite clear: I see your eyes as mocking and your hands as nervous, just as I see your eyes as brown and your hands as sinuous. I simply see them. But just as I see your eyes as mocking and your hands as nervous, I see you as human, and I cannot see you otherwise. Seeing a person as human does require that what we see in his body we see under mental labels (in a secondary sense), but this does not mean that the perceiver must be able to describe what she sees in mental terms. The perceiver may be inarticulate, and instead of describing what she sees verbally she may illustrate it in a painting, in a pantomime, or in some indirect verbal way from which we can infer that she sees the other humanly.

If seeing human beings as human is seeing them tagged with the labels of human psychology, what could constitute a continuing perception of humans as nonhuman?

What is blindness to the human aspect? Stephen Mulhall, who has investigated in depth the issue of seeing aspects, suggests explicating blindness to the human aspect as seeing in humans only what can be described in terms of color and form.[3] A human-blind person sees humans under a physical description without the capacity to see them under a psychological one. Such a person is not necessarily insensitive to human psychology, but for the human-blind person the human aspects of human beings are derived by reasoning rather than given by direct perception. A person with this handicap is like a blind person who knows that the car has stopped at the traffic light because the light is red and so deduces that the light must be red even though he cannot see it. The human-blind are not necessarily inhuman in their attitude to others—it depends on how they compensate for their human-blindness through reasoning.

If this is the meaning of human-blindness, then it is clear that it should be considered a pathological condition similar to color-blindness, except that what the person is blind to is the human aspect in human beings. Human-blindness is not a matter of choice or decision, just as color-blindness is not a voluntary matter. Even if we accept the suggested interpretation of seeing people as human and of human-blindness, however, we can still deny its importance for our general attitude toward humans. After all, nothing can compare with Rembrandt's paintings in causing us to see human beings in their human aspect, but we do not therefore believe that the blobs of paint on Rembrandt's canvases are humans, or that we must treat them as such. We hang Rembrandt's portrait of Jeremiah on the museum wall and consider this the appropriate attitude to the painting, although a similar treatment of Jeremiah himself would have been no less shameful than throwing him into the pit. Seeing a painting in its human aspect is totally different from seeing the human body in its human aspect. Seeing is not believing. I cannot help seeing the stick in the water as broken, but I am not therefore compelled to believe that it is broken. Then what is the point of seeing the human aspect, if this sort of perception can be applied to inanimate objects like canvases, and is not restricted to persons? What is the connection between seeing human beings as human and treating them as human, if seeing the human aspect is not necessarily something that applies only to human beings?

A human figure in a painting (like anything else in a painting) may be perceived in two different ways—as a figure internal to the picture and as a figure with an external reference. The painting of Rembrandt's mother can be evaluated in two different ways: by considering the painted figure without any connection to the mother herself, or by relating it to the figure external to the painting. Figures in a painting may not have any external connection, as when an artist paints out of his imagination and invents a figure without looking at a model. The question is what we identify as the figure outside the painting that is the external counterpart of the figure in the painting. Is it the historical Jeremiah that is the external figure associated with Rembrandt's painting, or is it the model Rembrandt used when painting his Jeremiah-picture? The external figure relevant for seeing the human aspect is the figure of the model.

There is a difference between seeing the human aspect of a figure external to a picture through its representation in the picture and seeing the human aspect of an internal figure. In the case of an external figure the picture expresses the soul of the figure in a way that can be seen as a natural extension of the bodily expressions of the figure itself. Even Gorbachev's facial expressions during his farewell speech were seen by most of us only on television. But although we did not see Gorbachev directly, what we saw was undoubtedly Gorbachev's expression. In the case of paintings of external figures the distance between the original and the observed figure is greater than that between the original and the image on the television screen, but the two are still on the same continuum. Even if the figure in the picture gets some of the reactions that are destined for the original external figure (the lover kisses the picture of the beloved), there is no fear of confusing the internal figure with the external one. The mother whose daughter's beauty is praised, and who responds, "Oh, that's nothing, you should see her picture," is ludicrous but not confused. At any rate, the sustained human aspect of a picture with an external reference to a human being is the external figure viewed through the picture. In that a picture is like a mirror.

The remaining question concerns pictures in which there is only an internal figure with no reference to a human being outside it. In such a case, who or what is seen as human? The question raises an implicit suspicion which ought to be made explicit. The opponents of idolatry often expressed the fear that representing the divinity by means of idols would lead to a situation in which the idols would be perceived as the divinity itself rather than merely its representations. This is the source of one of the justifications for the prohibition of idols. But does anyone really suspect that seeing a painting or statue as human might transfer to them attitudes appropriate only to human beings, so that the distinction between the figure and the image would be lost? There is no reason to believe that the fear that the god might be replaced by the idol has ever had any real basis—that is, that anyone has ever made the mistake of thinking that the idol was a god. I discuss this issue at length elsewhere.[4] But as far as the substitution of a person's picture for the person is concerned, it would seem that except for truly pathological cases, such as infatuated fetishists clinging to the statue of Nefertiti in the Egyptian Museum at Charlottenburg, a human-picture is not a human being. Even though we see pictures of humans as human, under normal conditions we are unable to avoid seeing the nonhuman aspects of these pictures as well, such as the form and the material out of which the picture is made, the fact that it is not made out of flesh and blood, and the fact that it is lifeless in the literal sense of the term. To wit, the human aspect of a human-picture cannot hide its nonhuman aspects.

More intriguing is the question of whether it is possible to see humans as beasts in the literal sense. Some of the psychological labels under which we see human beings are also apt for beasts, but we generally view human beings under (psychological) predicates that only they can sustain. Smiling is such an aspect. Lions, as Wittgenstein pointed out, cannot smile. We cannot say that a lion is smiling even if the corners of its mouth curve slightly upward and its eyes brighten.

One may object to the claim that only in pathological cases do people see other people as nonhuman in a sustained way: anyone who knows how "guys" stare at "dolls" knows that seeing humans in a nonhuman aspect is commonplace rather than exceptional. Men who see women only through the size of their breasts and the curve of their hips, the extent of their tan and the color of their hair, are blind to their human aspect. They see women purely in terms of colors and shapes; in other words, they are human-blind.

But is this really so? I am not denying that there are "guys" who see "dolls" in the way just described, but I claim that even the most vulgar of macho men do not see women only under sexual labels. They may assign the greatest weight to sexual appearance viewed in terms such as color and shape, volume and size, in informing their lust toward women, but I deny that they are blind to the human smile. The spectacle of "guys" staring at "dolls" is depressing on many counts, but not as an example of human-blindness in the literal sense of the term, which is the sense that concerns us here.

Ignoring Humans and Seeing Humans as Subhuman

I have denied the view that humiliation already takes place in the eyes of the one who sees the other as nonhuman. If the degrader were really capable—in a literal sense—of seeing the other as nonhuman, this would be, on the face of it, a weighty reason for the other to feel humiliated. But as a matter of fact the degrader does not necessarily see the other as nonhuman. Humans see others as human. This human aspect is not necessarily a humanitarian way of seeing—that is, seeing humans compassionately. A human way of seeing means seeing the other under the descriptions of human psychology. It means seeing the human body, especially the face and the eyes, as expressing psychological states. Seeing humans is not a matter of choice any more than seeing colors is. Just as there are partially or fully color-blind people, there are also people who are blind to the human aspect in others. The man who mistook his wife for a hat, in Oliver Sacks's fascinating case study, was blind in this way.[5] This man was very sick.

It is exceptional to see human beings as nonhuman. Yet it is easy to avoid seeing a person at all. This is an easy task whether it is intentional or nonintentional. Overlooking people does not necessarily mean turning one's gaze away in order to avoid seeing those one does not wish to see. Overlooking human beings means, among other things, not paying attention to them: looking without seeing. Seeing humans as ground rather than figure is a way of ignoring them. Seeing someone in this way is the same sort of avoidance that we sometimes call seeing a human being as an object, but this case doesn't really count as seeing the human involved as a thing. It is rather a case of not seeing the person or, more precisely, not paying attention to the person. The poet Denis Silk writes about "vanishing powder" that is sprinkled, so to speak, on Arabs from the occupied territories who work in Israel, a powder that makes them invisible: "A good Arab must work, not be seen."[6]

Overlooking the presence of the other is a recurrent theme in the anticolonialist literature of humiliation. The humiliation of the native is expressed in perceptual terms as seeing "through" the native as if he were transparent rather than seeing *him*. What does it mean to see "through" someone? One important sense is connected with seeing as normal what it is morally wrong to see as such. Seeing something as normal means seeing it as something that can be taken for granted. It means seeing things as "all right," as secure and stable. It is mixed up in our consciousness with the view that this is the way things are supposed to be. The normal allows us not to pay attention to details and to see our surroundings as familiar scenery that does not demand special examination, since it is assumed that things are the way they are supposed to be. What is humiliating for self-respecting natives in the colonialist experience is the fact that the humiliating masters see their surroundings as normal— that is, they do not see any signs of threat in the environment which should, in the view of the proud natives, be riddled with threatening signals to the masters on account of their oppression. The proud natives want to be taken as a threat by their masters and to see themselves as constituting such a threat in the masters' eyes. In the natives' view the masters ought to *be* threatened and, moreover, ought to *feel* threatened. If they do not feel threatened and everything seems normal to them, this is evidence of the natives' humiliating helplessness.

To try to see other people precisely, to pay attention to the changes in their expression and thereby to their feelings and moods, is to a large extent subject to our decision—that is, a voluntary matter. Ignoring other people can thus also be a voluntary act, and not only in extreme cases, such as when a person turns her head away from another in order not to see her, or covers her eyes with her hand in order to avoid seeing the other. Avoidance can also take the form of intentionally failing to try to see the other in detail. In situations where such an attempt is (normatively) expected, its absence takes on the meaning of seeing the other as an object. This is the way the masters of grand palaces saw their servants. They did not see them in detail. Not seeing servants in detail includes not seeing their gaze as an obstacle or limitation of any sort on the masters' behavior. One may fornicate in their presence—in essence, one may do anything whatsoever in front of them. The servants too are expected to put in the effort required to make it easy for their masters to safely ignore them. They are expected to exhibit a blank look, devoid of all interest in what is going on—that is, to act as though they see nothing, so that their gaze will not embarrass anyone. Hudson's instructions to the new servants in the Bellamy household on the television series "Upstairs Downstairs" include exact stage directions as to how the servants must behave: as if they are minding only their own limited business and ignoring everything else, so that the masters will be able to overlook them with ease.

Overlooking humans thus does not strictly mean seeing them as things, but rather not seeing them fully or precisely. But although people do not normally see others as objects, there are cases where people see others as subhuman. To see human beings as subhuman means to see them as stigmatized—that is, to see some physical "anomaly" of theirs as a sign of a defect in their humanity. This anomaly is not necessarily present in a part of their body, but may also be found in certain items of dress. People who cannot tolerate ultra-orthodox Jews see not only their beards and sidecurls as a stigma, but also their fur-trimmed hats. Similarly, the galabiya and the turban join the Assyrian beard as stigmata of Islamic fundamentalists. Prominent items of dress that people wear on a permanent basis can serve as marks of stigma just like bodily signs. And vision is not the only sense that can be used to define stigmata. Smell is also a powerful tool for lowering people to the status of subhumans—from the smell of their sweat to the odor of the onions, garlic, or curry they eat. But I focus here on vision rather than the other senses.

Stigmata serve as marks of Cain upon people's very humanity. Bearers of a stigma appear to their surroundings as bearers of a label that makes them seem less human. Although others continue to see them as human, they are viewed as stigmatized humans. Erwin Goffman stressed the injury to the social identity of those stigmatized,[7] but it seems to me that the main point is the injury to their very humanity. The stigmatized are seen as human beings, but as severely flawed human beings—in other words, as subhuman. The stigma denotes a serious deviation from the stereotype of the "normal appearance" of a human being. Dwarfs, amputees, people with burned faces, severe albinos, and extremely obese people are only some of the bearers of stigmata that distort our view of the other as human. When the stigma takes over—that is, overshadows the characteristics that allow us to see the other as human to such an extent that all our attention is focused on the fact of his being, say, a dwarf—then our seeing turns into seeing the other as subhuman. Sometimes directed efforts are made to bring the victims of aggression to a state where they can be seen as nonhuman, as in the case of the Muselman in the Nazi concentration camps. A humiliating look thus does not consist in seeing the other as a thing or a machine but in seeing the other as subhuman.

Such a way of looking at humans is possible, and it fits in with the central idea of humiliation as the rejection of a person or a group of people from the human commonwealth. This idea is addressed in Chapter 8. The focus here is on the perceptual aspect of rejection. Those who are looked at as subhuman have a reason—and perhaps even a sufficient reason—for considering themselves humiliated. This last point poses a moral problem. If indeed seeing humans as subhuman has to do with perception rather than interpretation, then how can the humiliators be faulted for what is not under their control, namely, the way they see things? Isn't this like blaming near-sighted people for their defect?

This question is disturbing even if it belongs more to the level of humiliation by individuals than to institutional humiliation. The answer to the question about the immorality of seeing humans as subhuman requires clarification of the relation between seeing and interpreting. The line I am taking here on this issue belongs to a larger picture whose contours are basically different from those in the accepted picture. The accepted picture of human behavior presents people as endlessly engaged with questions of decision—from the most trifling decisions, such as crossing a road, to the most momentous ones, such as choosing a life partner. All of these are perceived as decisions involving desires ("utilities") and beliefs ("subjective probabilities"). According to this view we never stop deciding and we are constantly assessing, weighing, and calculating.

As against this view, which sees a decision behind every act, I hold an alternative picture. On the whole, people do not make decisions. On the contrary, they put in considerable effort to avoid making decisions. They act mostly out of habit—that is, in a framework of standard procedures. Crossing the road is only rarely a problem that requires a decision. A call for decision generally arises only as a form of pathology when habitual procedures collapse, or when the stakes are particularly high and justify the effort of thinking. Decision is not the rule but the exception. There are people who live almost their entire lives without making decisions. They drift into various deeds, including important ones that perhaps do in principle require deliberation and decision. My claim is not that there are no decisions in our lives but that they occur much less often than we are led to believe by the picture of agents as decision makers.

The picture of people as interpreters is misleading in much the same way, since interpretation seems to me a special case of action on the basis of decision. Understanding, I maintain, is based on habit, not decision, whereas interpretation is based on hypotheses, on reasoning, on marshaling evidence—in short, on conscious, voluntary activity. The issue we were discussing is the contrast between seeing and interpreting in the context of perception. This contrast is not by any means identical with the one between looking at things with a naive, "naked" eye and looking at them with an intelligent, interpreting eye—that is, using one's intelligence in the act of looking. Seeing, especially seeing aspects, is a combination of perception and thought. What we see is affected by what we habitually expect to see. People who grew up in a racist society see stigmata where "color-blind" people do not. At the same time, people brought up to be racist also avoid seeing aspects that the "color-blind" do see and notice. The habit of seeing, especially the seeing of aspects, is also shaped by culture and history. The fact that seeing aspects is affected by the society in which it takes place does not make it a matter of interpretation. Seeing aspects may well be an acquired automatic type of seeing. This does not imply that all aspect-seeing is acquired—for example, seeing human beings as human is not acquired but innate. But seeing humans as subhuman is liable to be acquired—for example, Nazi education can bring people to see Jews and Gypsies as subhuman.

People cannot directly control what they see. They can do so indirectly through a conscious change in their attitude to the things they are seeing. The eye can be trained to ignore stigmata and to see people precisely in their human aspect. The fact that this cannot be done as a result of direct decision only means that it has to be accomplished indirectly.

In the case of visual illusions, such as the stick that looks broken in the water, we do not have the power, whether directly or indirectly, to avoid seeing the stick that way. The only thing we can do is not believe what we see. In contrast, seeing human beings as subhuman is not a perceptual illusion of this sort. Here we can change our perception itself, although, as mentioned, only indirectly. In the case of seeing a person in a humiliating subhuman aspect, we must take care not only to refuse to believe our eyes but also to try not to see—in the perceptual sense of seeing—the other as subhuman. What is needed is "a-stigmatic" vision.

The expression "seeing humans as one thing or another" has the idiomatic meaning of treating people in one way or another. But I have attempted in the last two sections to take this expression literally—that is, to use the word "seeing" in its strict sense.

Treating Humans as Subhuman

I claim that humiliation is the rejection of a human being from the "Family of Man"[8]—that is, treating humans as nonhuman, or relating to humans as if they were not human. Treating persons as if they were not human is treating them as if they were objects or animals. The important role of ceremonies or gestures of humiliation derives from the fact that humiliation involves acting toward persons "as if"—as if they were inanimate objects, as if they were tools, as if they were beasts. But these humiliating attitudes are not authentic. Authentic attitudes of rejection are based on treating persons as subhuman, as an inferior species of human beings. In contrast, attitudes of rejecting people from the community of humankind, as objects or animals, do not express an authentic attitude toward these people. The attitude is *as if* they were objects, *as if* they were beasts.

This convoluted way of presenting the issue stems from the fact that the attitudes under discussion are not simply false beliefs about other people, beliefs that some humans are not really human. The key word here should be "posture," which stands for a more basic attitude than belief. When I say that an attitude is more basic I do not mean that it is an unreflective reaction. If we formulate the content of the "posture" in words, sentences expressing postures are not those expressing beliefs. The role of posture-expressing sentences is that of framework sentences. Framework sentences constitute the rules of our representation of the world. To say that the other has a soul and is not a machine is to provide a framework for representing the other. This is what enables us to hold beliefs about other human beings—beliefs about what they want, what they feel, what they think. A sentence expressing a belief is a bipolar one: it is not enough that we know what in the world would make the sentence true, we must also know what it would mean for the sentence to be false. A framework sentence such as "She has a soul" is not bipolar. We do not know what it would mean for it to be false. That other human beings have souls—that is, are subjects of psychological predicates—is not a hypothesis but the provision of a framework for representing human beings as such. Framework sentences delineate the way to represent our objects. Holding framework sentences is an attitude that is not the result of a decision. This does not mean that adhering to framework sentences is an unchangeable posture, but that changes in posture do not take place as a result of decision.

This analysis has shifted our discussion from postures toward the other to postures toward framework sentences about the other. Let us return to the treatment of the other as human aside from the issue of attitudes toward sentences.

My central claim is that humiliation typically presupposes the humanity of the humiliated. Humiliating behavior rejects the other as nonhuman, but the act of rejection presupposes that it is a person that is being rejected. This claim is close to Hegel's account of the master-slave dialectic.[9] The master wants absolute power over the slave, but he also wants the slave to recognize his absolute power. The two desires are in conflict. The master's attitude here is similar to that of a soccer team that wants to defeat the rival side decisively but also wants its victory to be recognized as an achievement. A crushing victory decreases the value of winning since it testifies that the other side was not a worthy opponent. Here lies the contradiction—one wants and does not want to trounce one's rivals, at one and the same time. One wants to beat them hard in order to demonstrate one's decisive superiority, but one does not want to defeat them quite so crushingly, so that one's superiority is of value.

If we render the master-slave relationship in terms of humiliation and respect, then the master's humiliation of the slave is self-defeating. The victim must be taken as someone with awareness, thus possessing implicit human worth, in order for the act of humiliation which denies his humanity to take place. Humiliation is intended both to prove absolute superiority and to win recognition, which is a conceptual impossibility. Absolute superiority can be achieved only with regard to what is not human; recognition can be attained only from other humans.

The master-slave relationship provides us with a simple way of testing the assumptions on which humiliation is based. Manifestations of the institution of slavery—as it existed, for example, in ancient Rome and in the American South—attest that, however hard and cruel it was, such slavery was not based on the assumption that the slave was a mere object or just a draft horse. This does not mean that slaves were treated with greater mercy due to their humanness. Yet the children of the Southern slaves were baptized in church, and clearly no one believed plows or ponies were being baptized. It is true, of course, that the slaves were sold in the slave market, and it is also true that the prospective buyers inspected their teeth to see how healthy they were, just as they would do if they were considering buying a horse. The sale of slaves highlights the fact that they were considered as having exchange value, but the requirement that they be Christian attests to more than a glimmer of awareness of their humanity.

As for ancient Rome, Paul Veyne rightly claims that the way to describe how masters thought of their slaves is as human beings who are inherently immature and thus incapable of becoming adults.[10] An expression of this is the fact that in many languages the term for a male slave is "boy" ("puer" in Latin, "na'ar" in the Hebrew of the Bible, "boy" in the South). I view these linguistic expressions as betraying an attitude toward subhumans rather than nonhumans. On the one hand the slaves were seen under psychological predicates, but on the other hand these were predicates appropriate only for children. Veyne mentions that when Plautus wanted to amuse his audience he described a slave in love.[11] Ascribing full human feelings to slaves seemed as grotesque to his listeners as a complex, passionate love story taking place in a kindergarten might strike us. True, grownups in our culture do not treat children as subhuman; however, treating slaves or "natives" like children is rightly seen as treating them as subhuman. It means treating them like children who will never grow up and become responsible for their actions. Perhaps the parallel in our society is the attitude toward those with Down's syndrome. Such people seem subhuman to many, as tagged by their stigmatic "mongoloid" appearance. This appearance is associated with the view that people with Down's syndrome can never fully grow up.

I maintain that even settings horrifying in their cruelty

betray the fact that the people in charge know very well that they are dealing with human beings. The Japanese forced-labor camps for prisoners of war were known for their fearful ferocity, but it is reported that in one of these hideous camps the commander took his enslaved prisoners up the mountain to see the cherry blossoms. He felt that this wondrous sight could not be withheld from anyone, accursed as he might be. Nazi propaganda frequently compared Jews to rats: rats poison wells, while the Jews were perceived as "poisoners of culture." Yet a poisoner of culture cannot be a rat, in spite of Nazi propaganda to equate the two. Even Heinrich Himmler, the arch-racist, was forced to admit, in his famous speech before the SS commandants in Posnan, that killing people in camps is not the same as killing rats. Thus the killers' efforts to suppress their natural feelings toward the wretched were far more "heroic" than if they had merely been killing rats. The special cruelty toward the victims in the forced-labor and the death camps—especially the humiliations that took place there—happened the way it did because human beings were involved. Animals would not have been abused in the same way. For one thing, animals do not have accusing eyes.

Thus the basic claims are these: the key concept for humiliation is rejection from the human commonwealth. But such rejection is not based on a belief or attitude that the rejected person is merely an object or an animal. The rejection consists of behaving *as if* the person were an object or an animal. Such rejection typically consists in treating humans as subhuman.

III

*Decency as a Social
Concept*

7

The Paradox of Humiliation

There seems to be a competing notion of humiliation to that of rejection from human society. This is the notion of humiliation as the deliberate infliction of utter loss of freedom and control over one's vital interests. I maintain, however, that the idea of humiliation as rejection contains the idea of humiliation as loss of control. Yet each idea emphasizes a different perspective. Humiliation as rejection stresses the injurer's point of view, whereas humiliation as loss of control underlines the standpoint of the humiliated. But first we must clarify in what sense humiliation involves loss of control.

Sick or old people sometimes lose control over their bodily functions. This gives them a painful sense of loss of dignity. A central component of the sense of pride in oneself is a sense of self-control. Respect for self-control is also an important element of the respect others command in us. The Indian chief in the Western, who speaks in a composed tone of utter self-control, gives us the sense that he has impressive pride in himself. In the exhibition of social honor, as in the representation of personal dignity, gestures of self-control have a place of honor.

115

Self-control must be distinguished from self-discipline. Self-discipline is manifested in the control one exercises over one's actions in a specific area, with respect to a specific goal. An artisan may be capable of strict discipline in his work even when it involves the hardship of giving up immediate, or not-so-immediate, satisfactions for the sake of achieving professional perfection. The same artisan, however, may show an utter lack of self-control in his nonprofessional life. People who nourish cold revenge manifest self-discipline rather than self-control. Self-control is not tied to a specific goal—it is not confined to the Procrustean bed of some definite act.

Loss of self-respect as loss of self-control is related to the idea of self-respect as autarchy. A self-controlled person seems unaffected by external stimuli. But the distinction between external and internal stimuli is problematic. In one sense Don Quixote was reacting to windmills—an external stimulus—but he reacted to them under the description of knights' horses that came from his feverish brain—an "internal" stimulus. Yet in spite of the difficulty, the general idea is clear: self-control is manifested in delayed reactions, reflective rather than reflexive, to the external environment. It is expressed in overcoming one's "inner drives" by acting on the basis of reasons and not only on the basis of causes and motives. A considerable proportion of the most humiliating gestures are those which show the victims that they lack even the most minuscule degree of control over their fate—that they are helpless and subject to the good will (or rather, the bad will) of their tormentors.

But what is the connection between this and the idea that lack of control touches our central conception of humiliation as the rejection of human beings as human? Sartre provides us with a useful framework for discussing the connection between humiliation as lack of control—that is, lack of freedom—and humiliation as the rejection of human beings as human.

Seeing human beings in a human aspect, according to Sartre, means seeing them as free to make decisions bearing on their lives. Seeing a human being as a thing, as a "body," is seeing him as unfree. When a person denies his ability to be free (what Sartre calls "having bad faith"), we see him as behaving according to a tag attached to him from the outside. The waiter in Sartre's famous example behaves like a marionette of a waiter.[1] He does not behave under the aspect of humanness, but as if he were playing a role—as if his role had taken the place of his soul. We do not see the owner of a body or the player of a role in a fully human aspect as long as we see him merely in terms of his body or his role—in other words, as long as we do not see him as a free agent capable of making decisions about the conduct of his life.

I have already mentioned Sartre's view that human beings have no nature, but now I must hedge this claim. Humans have no nature in the sense that they have no set of "character" traits or tendencies that uniquely determine the course of their lives. Every human being has the radical possibility of starting life anew at any moment irrespective of his life's previous course. This freedom to shape one's life is, in another sense, the only nature humans have, in contrast to other animals and things. Humans have no character, but they do have a nature in this sense.

Such ambivalence about the meaning of the concept

"nature" is not new. Marx also denies that Man has a
nature and insists on Man's always having the capacity to
rebel. In other words, it is impossible to eradicate Man's
rebellious nature—it can only be temporarily paralyzed.
The assertion that humans are free beings is an ontologi-
cal assertion, like Descartes' characterization of matter as
having extension and of the soul as thinking. Treating
someone in a way that denies her capacity to be free is
rejecting her as a human being. The sadist treats his victim
as solely a body, not seeing her under the aspect of freedom—in other words, not seeing her in a human aspect.
The masochist, complementarily, is one who presents herself to her tormentor as entirely unfree. The name of the
game between the two is humiliation.

Relations between a sadist and a masochist, especially
of a sexual kind, involve an inhuman attitude toward the
fettered victim as someone who allows her molester to act
out his fantasies of omnipotence. As in the master-slave
relationship, it turns out that this is a self-defeating attitude. An aspirant to omnipotence needs to have his absolute superiority recognized. Such recognition has value
only if it comes from a free agent, that is, a full-fledged
person. This being so, much treatment of humans as
nonhuman is "as-if." This means that the treatment does
not really deny the humanness of the other on an onto-
logical level. It denies the other's freedom on the level of
the concrete relations between them. Curtailing the freedom of the other, and making gestures designed to show
that the other is severely limited in her control, may
constitute a rejection of the other as human. Such is the
connection between humiliation as rejection and humiliation as utter lack of control.

One might ask how this idea of humiliation as taking away human freedom—that is, preventing people from making decisions concerning vital interests of theirs—fits in with the picture presented earlier, of humans as making every effort to avoid decisions. The answer is that there is no logical or practical contradiction between the picture of humans as acting in their everyday life on the basis of habits and standard procedures requiring no decisions, and the picture of a human being as free to make decisions if and when she chooses to do so, in spite of the existence of these habits and routines.

Back to our main concern. The basic claim of this section is that humiliation as a severe diminution of human freedom and control is subsumed under the idea of humiliation as the rejection of human beings as human. This is true under the assumption that rejecting human beings as human means rejecting them as beings capable of freedom, since it is freedom that makes them humans rather than mere things.

I have discussed the connection between two concepts of humiliation—humiliation as rejection from the human commonwealth and humiliation as extreme injury to the other's control over herself. But whichever of these concepts is adopted, the notion of humiliation leads to a paradox. I discuss this paradox in the next section.

The Insult and Humiliation Paradoxes

The words "insult" and "humiliation" are on a continuum. Humiliation is an extreme case of insult, while both of them denote injury to one's honor. This book, however, makes a qualitative distinction between the two. "Insult"

denotes injury to one's social honor; "humiliation" denotes injury to one's self-respect. Insults may injure the
offended person's self-esteem. Humiliation injures one's
sense of intrinsic value.

The paradox of humiliation may be expressed graphically as follows: if the mark of Cain is stamped on Cain's
forehead then there is nothing wicked about it, because
Cain deserves it. And if the mark of Cain is stamped on
Abel's forehead by mistake, Abel ought not to take it too
hard, since he knows very well that he has not shed blood.
He should not think badly of himself just because the
mark of Cain was mistakenly stamped on his forehead.

Insult is a social evil because of the ill it causes to the
offended one in the eyes of others. But if humiliation, in
contrast, involves supplying victims with a sound reason
for viewing their self-respect as having been injured, it
seems to lack any raison d'être. For if, as mentioned, the
humiliation is merely justified criticism, then it should
change the way people evaluate themselves without damaging their self-respect. And if it is unjustified, then it
should not even diminish their self-esteem, let alone damage their self-respect. The humiliation paradox returns us
in essence to the Stoic critique that it is never rational to
feel humiliated. That is, people may be humiliated in a
psychological sense, but not in a normative sense.

Bernard Williams distinguishes between "red" and
"white" emotions—that is, emotions that make us blush
and emotions that make us pale. Shame is a red emotion;
guilt is a white emotion. A red emotion is an emotion in
which one sees herself through the eyes of the other, and
therefore blushes. In a white emotion the person sees

herself with the "inner eyes" of her conscience, which may make her pale. One's point of view in the two types of emotions is different. The paradox of humiliation is that on the one hand the person sees herself through the eyes of others—the bullies—yet on the other hand the normative sense of humiliation is that she is to respond from her own point of view. Humiliation is a red emotion, yet the victim assumes a response which fits a white emotion. A person's face cannot be red all over and white all over at the same time.

Insult, by definition, depends on the attitude of the other, since it involves an injury to the person's social honor. If the insult is based on a false charge, yet the insulted one has reason to believe that, false or not, he will have to pay with his social honor, then he has good reason to be insulted. But in the case of an unjustified act of humiliation—and any attempt to humiliate a person is unjustified—the question is whether the victim has a sound reason for considering himself humiliated, that is, for considering his self-respect to have been diminished in his own eyes.

Let us sharpen the question. Humiliation is the rejection of human beings as human, that is, treating people as if they were not human beings but merely things, tools, animals, subhumans, or inferior humans. It is easy to see why such "as if" treatment is liable to be insulting and shaming—that is, excessively damaging to people's social honor. But why should such treatment provide the victims with a reason for considering themselves devalued in their worth human beings? Why should they adopt the point of view that the humiliating bully is trying to get them to adopt? That victims tend to identify with their tormentors is regarded as a psychological fact, but our question is normative, not psychological.

Humiliation involves an existential threat. It is based on the fact that the perpetrator—especially the institutional humiliator—has power over the victim he assails. It crucially involves the sense of utter helplessness that the bully gives the victim. This sense of defenselessness manifests itself in the victim's fear of impotence in protecting vital interests of hers. Even if the humiliated person attempts to turn the tables and see her tormentor—in the nonliteral sense of seeing—as a beast, this should not mitigate her feeling of humiliation. Humiliation coming from a human monster, such as Mengele, is indeed humiliation. The victim perceives the existential threat in the humiliating acts and is aware of her own helplessness in the face of this threat. Even if she succeeds in convincing herself that the "handsome devil" on the platform, as Mengele appeared to his victims, is really a devil and not a human being, she has not rid herself of the justified awareness of the humiliation in her situation. The humiliation exists, and it is justified, since the victim cannot help seeing Mengele as human. The tactic of seeing Mengele as a wild beast and thus not seeing his actions as a reason for humiliation is just that—a tactic. My claim is that even if the tactic worked, the humiliating situation would remain. Humiliation, as the rejection of human beings as human, even if it is performed ritually or symbolically without any physical cruelty, serves as a signal of existential rejection that is not symbolic at all. There is a constant threat of living a life unworthy of a human being.

During their long history of survival in the Diaspora,

Jews often assumed an attitude toward Gentiles that considered the latter to be "barking dogs." No one need be insulted or humiliated by them; after all, no one is insulted or humiliated by a barking dog. The dog may be frightening, never humiliating. This attempt by victims of humiliation to dehumanize their tormentors, understandable as it is, is not entirely unlike the bullies' attempt to dehumanize their victims.

Another device used by Jews throughout the centuries is the "Good Soldier Schweik" technique, the adoption of an attitude of mock innocence toward the potential tormentor—an attitude that avoids taking the bully seriously by making him a ridiculous figure. Yet it would seem that this option is always available, and so the question is why humiliation should ever be taken seriously. The existential threat implicit in the humiliation must be taken seriously, but not the humiliation itself. The victim has no reason to see any flaw in his human value, but only a danger to his existence, or to his basic human condition.

But all these defensive tricks of the weak in humiliating situations—the "barking dog" tactic, the "Good Soldier Schweik" technique, turning a badge of shame into a badge of honor, as in "Black is beautiful," or the denial tactic of "He's not spitting on me, it's only raining"—cannot uproot the humiliating situation. At most they may mitigate it somewhat.

But, again, why is this so? Why is it rational to consider yourself humiliated? Society is a prerequisite for social honor, but only you are needed to bestow self-respect upon yourself. If this is the case, then how can strangers, whether individuals or a group, determine whether and how you should respect yourself? Moreover, self-respect is the respect you confer upon yourself as a human being. It is not based on any evaluation of yourself for any sort of achievement. Being human is a feature, not a relation. Being human is not dependent in any way on what anyone thinks about you, or how anyone treats you, just as your having bushy hair is not a feature dependent on anyone's attitude or on what anyone thinks about your hair. Even if other people laugh at your hair, saying it is thinning, this ridicule does not give you a sound reason for feeling or believing that you are losing your hair, if in fact it is still bushy.

One answer to this query is: although self-respect is an attitude you may have toward yourself, it depends on the attitude of others toward you. This dependence is not merely causal—it does not consist only of the fact that what people think of you, and the way they treat you, affect your own attitude toward yourself psychologically. The dependence is conceptual as well.

The skeptical justification for respecting human beings is rooted in the fact that we all recognize one another as part of humanity and for this reason and this reason alone we deserve respect. As mentioned, the skeptical justification is based from the outset on an attitude rather than a trait. Any traits that might be used to justify respect are parasitic on our attitude toward human beings as human. Thus any attempt to reject a person from the human commonwealth erodes the base on which respect is founded. Even if the humiliated person has no doubt that she has incurred an appalling injustice, whereas she is just as human as anyone else, she cannot ignore how others treat her in shaping the way she regards herself. This is because the attitude of others, however base they may be, is required for determining what defines the common-wealth of mankind—a commonwealth that there is value in belonging to. The attitude of others is built into the very concept of the value of humans which the bearer of self-respect is supposed to adopt with regard to herself. All in all, someone with self-respect is not exempt from taking into account the attitude of other people toward her.

There are important issues in philosophy where structural problems crop up in which cases that on the surface do not appear to require reference to things outside themselves turn out under analysis to require such reference after all. Thus, for example, Hume's analysis of causality is based on the idea that one event is the cause of another only if events of the first type are always accompanied by events of the second type. But why do we need these other events of the same type? If there were only one window-pane in the world, and only one stone, wouldn't the throwing of this stone at that windowpane be the cause of the window's breaking even if there were no other cases of stone-throwing or broken windows in the world? According to the analysis given by Hume, who believes that causality is in the way we view things and not in the "world," other events are necessary in order for us to be able to create the concept of causality. This concept is a psychological product of conditioning, and in Hume's view there is no conditioning on the basis of one stimulus. This is true of all general terms, such as "red." "Red" may be defined, say, as whatever is the same color as my spilled blood. But isn't it possible that my spilled blood might be the only red thing in the universe? Here too the concept of red could not be formed if there were only one red thing in the world. The same sort of argument suggests that my language would also be impossible if I did not know that others share it. Indeed, there is a whole battery of philosophical arguments in which it seems at first that there is a concept that could be applied to only one thing in the world, without anything else having to exist, yet under scrutiny it turns out that the formation of such a concept calls for the existence of other things. Likewise, self-respect, although based on one's human worth in one's own eyes, implicitly assumes the need for other respectful human beings.

Divine Honor and Human Dignity

It may be helpful to compare the concept of human dignity with the notion of divine honor in the monotheistic religions. God, in these religions, is jealous of His honor. God demands to be honored even by people who have proved by their actions—the worship of other gods—that they are not worthy of honoring Him. God's zeal for His honor is odd since the other gods are considered worthless and insubstantial, yet it is precisely these nonentities that the foolish idolaters choose to worship. What is the point of requiring the followers of these "broken cisterns" to worship the source of the "living waters"? Why demand the honor of the One and Only God from a community of fools and evildoers? Can God and His "self-respect" be dependent on such people?

The conclusion to be drawn from this argument is the blunt statement that if the Great and Terrible God requires the affirmation of human beings, then other human beings require it all the more. The biblical God requires even those who are least worthy of worshiping and honoring Him to preserve His honor. Out of *imitatio Dei* we can say that the psychological fact that we find ourselves humiliated—perhaps degraded is a better word in this case—even by the lowest of the low is a fundamental fact of our lives. The attempt to find a general justification for this fact is ludicrous. That's the way it is, that's life. Of course, in certain instances we may ask someone to justify why he considers himself humiliated by something that no one else considers humiliating—for example, if it really is raining and he believes someone is spitting on him. But to ask why the Jews in the Viennese square considered themselves degraded when their Nazi tormentors forced them to scrub the pavement is absurd. If that is not humiliation, then what is?

But there is another way of understanding God's need to be honored even by those who are not worthy of honoring Him. This is an interpretation of the need for honor through a paradox complementary to the humiliation paradox—namely, the paradox of love. The lover, in sharp contrast to the humiliator, sees the object of his or her love as human. Treating the beloved as human means accepting the other as having freedom of choice. On the one hand the lover wants to appropriate the beloved exclusively for himself, but on the other hand he wants her to choose him freely. Even if she does choose him, however, he remains full of anxiety that she may one day stop loving him. Thus he finds himself in a state of sharp tension between the desire for absolute control over the beloved in order to keep her exclusively his and the opposite desire that the other, the beloved, should remain free to choose, even though this endangers the lover's exclusivity. (This, for example, is how Sartre interprets Proust's Albertine.) God wants to be loved and honored exclusively, but this love and worship have value only if they come from beings with the power to choose, including making exceedingly mistaken choices, even the choice of worshiping nonentities.

These paradoxes attest that there is a self-defeating element in the enterprises of love and humiliation. This is not a logical contradiction which would make it impossible to love or to humiliate anyone. It is rather a conceptual tension that raises the question of whether love and humiliation are emotions that can be justified, and not merely caused. I have been arguing that one may justifiably feel hurt when rejected in love in favor of a good-for-nothing, and one may justifiably feel humiliated by someone worthless.

Humiliation is a clearer case than love, since humiliation can be felt even in the absence of a humiliating agent. It is possible to be humiliated by one's life conditions, provided they are man-made. This has no parallel in love. Humiliation does not require a humiliator, and so it is less important to find out who the humiliators are than to ascertain whether there is a justification for feeling humiliated. In our case, since we are concerned with institutional humiliation—whose agents are clerks, police, soldiers, prison wardens, teachers, social workers, judges, and all the other agents of authority—we can ignore the subjective intentions of the humiliators in examining whether their actions are degrading. This is especially justified when we are discussing systematic humiliation that is not the whim of a particular individual in authority. It is easy to see systematic institutional humiliation as a degrading situation, while disregarding the question of whether the humiliators as individuals are significant enough to justify one's feeling humiliated.

Shifting the discussion from humiliating agents to a humiliating situation is not intended to absolve those actually doing the humiliating on behalf of the institutions from their individual moral responsibility for their deeds. It is meant rather to remove the obstacle in understanding why it is rational for victims of humiliation to consider themselves degraded. The shift from a humiliating agent to a humiliating situation is important because institutional humiliation is independent of the peculiarities of the humiliating agent, depending only on the nature of the humiliation. It thus contrasts with the sort of humiliation that takes place in personal relations. You do not have to value the official humiliating you in order to value the institution she is serving. Moreover, you do not even have to value the institution in order to recognize its power to create degrading conditions. Love, unlike humiliation, cannot be shifted from an individual to an institution. Institutions do not love.

8

Rejection

If a decent society is a nonhumiliating society, does this mean it is also a nonshaming society? In other words, does it also have to be a society whose institutions do not shame those in its orbit? Moreover, is it also a nonembarrassing society?

One distinction which has gained currency is that between shame societies and guilt societies. The axis of the distinction passes between societies whose members internalize the society's norms, so that when they disobey these norms they feel guilt, and societies where everything is externalized and the predominant motive of its members is to avoid external sanctions and maintain their honor and good name in the eyes of others, lest they feel shame. It seems that according to this rough distinction the shame society has very little to do with the decent society, since the latter is not concerned with the social honor of persons but only with their self-respect. If this is the case, then decent societies can be found only among guilt societies and not among shame societies. Shame societies can be decent ones in the sense of giving each person the honor he or she deserves, but they cannot be decent societies in the sense of giving each person equal respect as a human being. Humiliation in a shame society can only take the form of demotion—lowering people in the social hierarchy in such a way that they feel shame with regard to the others. This is not humiliation in the sense of damaging the person's self-respect. People in an ideal type of shame society have no sense of respect in and of themselves, only a sense of honor in the eyes of others. The idea that a person can perform a disgraceful act that no one but she knows about, and as a result can change her self-image for the worse, diminishing her stature as a human being, is alien to a shame society. What others don't know "doesn't exist" and so cannot be a source of shame.

Gabrielle Taylor writes about a boy who boasted to his friends about his conquests of girls which had never occurred,[1] the truth being that he was still a virgin. This boy might feel guilt for deceiving his friends, but he feels ashamed within himself for being a virgin. He lies to avoid being shamed by his friends, but this does not mean that he does not also feel ashamed within himself. What we can learn from this example is that the distinction between shame and guilt does not lie in the fact that shame is an external reaction while guilt is an internal reaction. The accepted characterization of guilt and shame societies is based on the contrast between "internal" and "external." The right way of looking at the distinction, however, is to see it as the difference between a person who sees his shameful acts or his failures from his own point of view and a person who sees them from the point of view of others. These others do not necessarily have to exist. In the case of others who no longer exist, the boundary

between guilt and shame is blurred. If a young Jew re-
nounces her faith and eats nonkosher food, might she feel
ashamed at the thought of her deceased observant parents, or might she feel guilty? It's not easy to tell.

Shame and humiliation are both "red" emotions in the
sense of involving the point of view of others. But just as
the existence of others may be a prerequisite for acquiring
self-awareness without preventing us from eventually
reaching an independent consciousness, so the fact that
we need the point of view of others in acquiring self-respect should not stop us from reaching a sense of respect
for ourselves which no longer depends on others.

If so, what is the difference between shame and humiliation? Shame, I submit, includes humiliation, but not vice
versa. This relation of inclusion needs to be clarified. The
class of flowers includes the class of roses. Whatever is a
rose is a flower, but not vice versa. In contrast, the concept
of a rose includes the concept of a flower, because the
definition of a rose includes the property of being a flower
as one of its properties, but not vice versa. There is an
inverse relation between inclusion in terms of classes (extension) and inclusion in terms of properties (intension).
The class of shaming events includes the class of humiliating events, but the concept of shame is included in the
concept of humiliation. Someone who is humiliated is also
shamed, but not necessarily the other way around.

One may feel ashamed of poor achievement, but on my
account this is not humiliation. Humiliation is not an
achievement concept. Shame involves humiliation only
when one is ashamed of a feature of her self-definition
connected with her belonging to a group. If a society,
through its institutions, causes people to feel ashamed of

a legitimate "belonging" feature of their self-definition—
for instance, being Irish, or Catholic, or a native of the
Bogside area of Belfast—then it is not a decent society. If
a person is ashamed of his parents or social origin, being,
for instance, the child of peasants ("kulaks")—which may
constitute important elements of his identity—and this
shame is brought about by the society's policies and institutional behavior, then the society is not a decent one.

Not every feature of one's self-definition is a morally
legitimate characteristic. A society which causes people to
feel ashamed for belonging to a crime syndicate, or a
society which causes Satan-worshipers engaged in sadistic
rites to feel ashamed of their "religion," should not be
accused of failing to be a decent society because it shames
such people. A society which causes the children of an
active Nazi to feel ashamed of their father need not lose
its claim to be a decent society. A society does lose this
claim if it causes the Nazi's children to feel guilty. They
may be justly caused to feel responsible, in the sense that
they ought to feel the need to compensate for their parent's actions, but they should not be made to feel guilty.
I thus distinguish between morally legitimate and illegiti-
mate aspects of a person's identity.

Another distinction is that between identity traits and
achievement traits. Shaming a person for legitimate identity traits is an act of humiliation. Shaming a person for
achievement aspects of his identity—for example, describing a writer as a hack when he defines himself as a great
poet—may be an insult, but it does not constitute humiliation. At least it does not provide a reason for feeling
humiliated, in the sense of moral degradation we are
using here.

Self-definition means the definition of a person's self-identity. Three different elements come under the heading of self-identity:

1. Personal identity—the conditions assuring that it is the same person at different time periods.
2. Identity of personality—the conditions assuring that the same person at different times also constitutes the same personality.
3. Personal identification—what this person identifies with over the long term. When psychologists such as Erik Erikson describe the identity crisis of adolescence, they are generally referring to this third notion of self-identity—mainly to the crisis of identification with one's parents or with their values.

A person's self-definition is centered mainly on identity of personality and personal identification. In Chapter 3 I discussed the concept of the inner wholeness of the personality—namely, integrity. I emphasized the aspect of faithfulness to your own principles and ideals, and the values by which you shape your life. A society is not decent, I claimed, if it compromises the integrity of its members. Here we are adding another important sense of integrity: the sense of being faithful to your self-definition, which is intended to assure the continuity of your life story over and above your personal identity. Self-definition is the way you make sure your life story remains continuous, even if it undergoes profound changes. In other words, even if there are discontinuities in your life—Trotskyite yesterday, conservative today—your life story is what integrates them.

Not all the elements of one's self-definition are equally important. I claim that it is precisely the features of belonging that are of particular significance. When a society rejects legitimate belonging features as disqualifying, it thereby disqualifies any person who identifies himself through them. It rejects the identity that the person sees as his own. In the following section I take up the idea of belonging to groups that play an important if not crucial role in one's personal identity and the identity of one's personality. Belonging to such groups also shapes the style in which the person expresses his personality (and other aspects of his self). Causing persons to feel ashamed of belonging to such a group (or groups) can be considered a rejection of their humanity and not only of their belonging to a particular group. In this sense causing persons to feel ashamed of what is morally legitimate belonging constitutes humiliation. I elaborate on this below.

So far the relation between the shame society and the decent society has been presented from the point of view of the victim. But perhaps the connection between shame and humiliation needs to be seen from the point of view of the humiliator. The idea here is that a decent society is one that has not lost its sense of shame—that is, a society whose members are ashamed of acts of humiliation and abuse.

Humiliation as Rejection from Encompassing Groups

I have characterized humiliation as rejection from humanity, or, somewhat sentimentally, from the "Family of Man." The difficulty with this idea is that the attempt to translate it into political and social terms creates the impression that it is too abstract and hence inapplicable in practice. After all, what in our own societies should be considered rejection from the human commonwealth? It seems that the only way to illustrate this notion of humiliation is by appeal to extreme cases of societies with concentration camps, forced-labor camps, or even extermination camps. In such cases, fearful humiliation obviously takes place, and it is easy to see how this constitutes rejection from humanity. But in the horrifying circumstances of such "camps," the problem of humiliation seems secondary to the physical cruelty. Survival takes priority over dignity. Self-respect seems like a luxury when life itself is at stake.

Yet there are survivors of these camps who insist that the humiliation they underwent there was the worst part of their suffering. It seems, however, that the survivors who considered humiliation their worst hardship probably form a biased sample—for one thing, they survived. It is also likely that those who were able to write about their memories of that hell were those most sensitive to the pain of humiliation. That is, it is reasonable to assume a positive correlation between writers of memoirs and people who are sensitive to symbolic gestures even in situations of severe bodily suffering. I see this fact as significant because we are inclined to exaggerate the importance of ideals and social values on the basis of the sample of those capable of writing about them. The latter often tip the balance toward values and ideals which have less weight among nonwriters. It so happens that nonwriters are the overwhelming majority. A clear example of this sort of bias is the significance of freedom, especially freedom of expression, among such people. Free speech is of utmost importance to writers, but nonwriters might perhaps prefer free time.

Yet humiliation, including the institutional sort, is very widespread. There is no need to look for violence-filled prisons, let alone faraway forced-labor camps, to discover its manifestations. Everyday examples of humiliation, however, do not usually constitute acts or attitudes that can be directly described as the rejection of human beings as human. What is more common in normal societies is mediated rejection. This is expressed in the rejection of groups that the person belongs to, groups that determine the way the person shapes her life as a human being. This issue came up in the preceding discussion of societies that shame their members for features of their self-definition—features such as nationality, religion, race, gender, and the like. A decent society is one that does not use its institutions to reject those in its orbit from belonging to legitimate encompassing groups. That is, it does not reject the groups, and it does not reject anyone who belongs to them owing to this fact. Before I explicate the concept of an encompassing group, here is the claim that this concept is meant to serve: humiliation is the rejection of legitimate encompassing groups. This definition of humiliation makes the concept more concrete and more applicable to societies familiar to us. We no longer need to look for "camps" or prisons to find evidence of humiliation—it is at our doorstep.

The questions we must now answer are: What is an encompassing group? And what is the connection between the concept of an encompassing group and the notion of humiliation as the rejection of human beings as human?

The term 'encompassing groups' appears in a joint essay by Joseph Raz and myself.[2] Here it serves a different but related purpose. In our article Raz and I delineated the notion of an encompassing group as follows:

1. An encompassing group has a common character and a common culture that encompasses many important and varied aspects of life. The common culture shapes its members' life styles, modes of action, aspirations, and relationships. In cases where the encompassing group is a nationality, we can expect there to be a national cuisine, a particular architectural style, a common language, a literary tradition, national music, customs, dress, ceremonies, festivals, and the like. None of these is mandatory, but they are the outstanding features that make a group an encompassing one. What is involved, then, is a group whose culture stands out, encompasses many aspects of life, and covers important and varied areas of its members' lives, especially those significant for the well-being of the people belonging to the culture.

2. A characteristic connected with (1) is that people growing up in the group acquire the group culture and possess its special traits. Their taste is noticeably influenced by the society's culture, and so are their choices: the types of careers available to them, their leisure activities, the customs and habits that color their relationships with other people—both friends

and strangers—and the patterns of expectations between couples and among other family members. All these are marked by the life styles emphasized in the group.

3. Membership in the group is partly a matter of mutual recognition. People are typically considered members of the group if they are identified as belonging to it by the other members of the group. Other conditions, such as birth, or belonging to the culture, are generally considered reasons for such identification. Encompassing groups are not formal settings with clear, explicit rules for membership. Membership is generally a matter of informal recognition by the other members.

4. Characteristic (3) paves the way for an explanation of the claim that membership in the group is important for the self-identification of those belonging to it. Membership in an encompassing group goes hand in hand with the identification of the members as belonging to the group. Belonging to the group is thus the accepted way for people to present themselves to others. The encompassing group has a salient presence in the larger society. Belonging to the group is an important fact for the members' self-understanding, but it is no less important for the members to be able to discuss their group affiliation with others outside the group so that the others should understand and sympathize with them.

5. Membership in the group is a matter of belonging rather than achievement. One need not prove oneself or excel in anything in order to be accepted as a full member in an encompassing group. Although affilia-

tion typically means recognition by others that one is a member of the group, it is not based on achievement. Being a prominent member of the group may be a matter of achievement, but just belonging is not. To be a good Irishman, as already mentioned, is a matter of achievement. Being Irish is solely a matter of belonging.

Belonging is generally determined by criteria that are not the result of choice. People do not decide to belong to an encompassing group. They belong because of what they are. The fact that membership in the group is based on belonging rather than achievement makes it a focus for identification because one's very membership in the group cannot be threatened the way it can in groups based on achievement.

6. Encompassing groups are not small face-to-face groups in which the members of the group know each other personally. They are anonymous groups. This makes it necessary to have a whole range of symbols— ceremonies, rituals, and other events and accessories— that enable the members to identify friends and foes.

These six characteristics of encompassing groups do not entail one another, but they tend to cluster together. And the way things are in our world, everyone belongs to an encompassing group, and generally to more than one— for example, nationality, Nigerian; tribe, Ibo; religion, Anglican.

Ridicule, hatred, oppression, or discrimination directed at encompassing groups in a given society are often a source of hurt, humiliation, degradation, moral abasement, and insult—as well as a reason for feeling hurt for people who belong to these groups and identify themselves through them. Hurting an encompassing group is liable to lower its members' self-image. This is true even if belonging to the group is not a matter of achievement. One important cause of this lowered self-image is the fact that group members are deprived of the sense of reflected glory they get from the achievements of successful members of their group. But we are interested in the damage to self-respect rather than to self-esteem.

Humiliation is the rejection of an encompassing group or the rejection from such a group of a person with a legitimate right to belong to it. A religious grouping, an ethnic minority, a social class, and the like are all liable to be rejected by the society as a whole in various ways and with various degrees of force—from being subject to ridicule to being totally banned, with heavy penalties for belonging to them. A decent society is one that does not reject morally legitimate encompassing groups. The reason for the restriction to legitimate groups is clear. The "underworld" may well satisfy the requirements for being an encompassing group. Circumstances can easily be imagined in which belonging to the underworld could be a source of identification and identity for its members, including people without any "achievements" in the world of crime, who just hang around with criminals. A decent society has not only a right but a duty to reject the underworld as an encompassing group.

But what about a homosexual group that serves as an encompassing group for its members? Can a society that forces such a homosexual group to "stay in the closet" be considered a decent society? The question is not whether it permits gays to be such in private, as a sort of secret society (a "Homintern," in Maurice Bawra's witty epithet). The question is what we should say of a society that forbids people to belong to a gay group as an encompassing group with overt signs of affiliation.

A decent society is not necessarily a respectable society. It must not restrict the formation of encompassing groups on a sexual basis. It is permissible for a decent society to ban immoral aspects of sexual behavior, such as the exploitation of minors. A society may place restrictions on the participation of minors in a gay group as an encompassing group without this preventing the society from being considered a decent one. But preventing the formation of encompassing groups on the basis of sexual behavior between consenting adults is humiliating on the face of it.

The function of encompassing groups can also be presented another way—adverbially. In other words, belonging to an encompassing group provides an adverb for describing the way people act and live their lives. Belonging to an encompassing group—being Irish, for instance—means doing certain things Irishly, being a Catholic means doing certain things Catholically, being a member of the proletariat means living proletarianly, and so on. A person can adopt several of these life styles simultaneously—for example, living Irishly, Catholically, and proletarianly.

Is it possible to be human without the stamp of at least one encompassing group? There is an interesting analogy here to stylistic genres in painting. It is possible to be just a painter, without any particular characterization of the way one paints. This is an appropriate description of an eclectic artist, but artists are generally described in different periods of their life according to the style of their paintings during that period. Some are abstract artists, other are figurative. Some are lyrical, others are brutal. There can be lyrical abstract artists and lyrical figurative artists, as well as all sorts of other combinations. All of these are ways of being artists. Analogously, there are different styles of being human, of expressing one's humanity. This is the deep sense of "Le style c'est l'homme même." Yet just as there are eclectic artists, there are also cosmopolitan people who do not belong to any encompassing group.

Different encompassing groups reflect different ways of being human. Rejecting a human being by humiliating her means rejecting the way she expresses herself as a human. It is precisely this fact that gives content to the abstract concept of humiliation as the rejection of human beings as human.

On the level of encompassing groups we may detect not only humiliation in the form of rejecting a whole group, but also in the form of ignoring the group, even if this is done through "benign neglect." Thus we must add that rejecting a person includes ignoring the person as well. The concrete ways in which people are rejected through the rejection of the encompassing groups they belong to is the main subject matter of Part III.

Justifications for Respect and the Elements of Humiliation

In Chapters 3 and 4, I discussed three types of justification for respecting human beings as human: (1) a positive justification based on the human capacity for repentance;

(2) a skeptical justification based on the idea that humans do not have any trait that justifies respect, but that there is an attitude of respect for humans in virtue of which the property of being human (skeptically) justifies respect; and (3) a negative justification that does not justify respect for humans but only the need to avoid humiliating people, because humiliation is a type of cruelty that can be directed only at human beings and cruelty of any sort is wrong.

In parallel, Chapter 6 discusses three elements that constitute humiliation, or, if you will, three senses of the term 'humiliation': (1) treating human beings as if they were not human—as beasts, machines, or subhumans; (2) performing actions that manifest or lead to loss of basic control; and (3) rejecting a human being from the "Family of Man."

This section explores some of the relations between the justifications for respecting humans and not humiliating them, on the one hand, and the three senses of humiliation, on the other. It also describes the connections among the various senses of humiliation.

The mediating factor between the justification for respect on the basis of the capacity for repentance and the concept of humiliation as loss of control is the concept of human freedom. The capacity for repentance is anchored in a Sartrean sense of freedom, which claims that a human being—if he wants to—can act radically differently from the way he acted in the past. To be sure, the sense in which humans can act differently if they want to requires more than will and ability on their part—it also requires opportunity. A criminal in prison has very little opportunity to lead the life of an upright citizen. Treating criminals with respect does not necessarily mean providing them with the opportunity to lead such a life by letting them out of prison. The respect they deserve is based on the possibility that they may repent—that they may show by words and deeds that they are capable of changing their lives and are willing to do so. The question of whether to provide them with the opportunity is another issue entirely.

The concept of freedom is thus a vector concept: it is the resultant of two forces, capacity and will. The two scholastic notions of freedom, freedom of spontaneity (an act is free if it is in accordance with the agent's will) and freedom of indifference (an act is free if it could have been done otherwise), are complementary concepts of freedom as requiring both capacity and will. Each of these concepts has a different focus—the first stresses will, while the second stresses capacity.

Even though the concept of repentance is formulated in terms of the capacity for radical change in one's life, the focus is actually more on the will than on the capacity. That is, the focus is on one's willingness to live differently as a result of a reevaluation of one's past life as the wrong sort of life to lead. In contrast, the concept of self-control, and the parallel concept of the loss of control that involves humiliation, relate to the notion of freedom as ability. The prototypical examples of loss of control as loss of the ability to act are being bound, being imprisoned, and being drugged. Loss of control in the present context involves mainly limitations on freedom in Isaiah Berlin's sense—that is, radical external intervention in a human being's ability to move about. We are not speaking here about injury to one's self-control in the thick positive sense of the freedom to shape one's life for the purpose of self-fulfillment.[3]

These three concepts of humiliation—treating humans as nonhuman, rejection, and acts intended to lead to lack of control or to highlight one's lack of control—are three different senses of the term 'humiliation.' These three senses are not three different meanings. A word is said have different 'senses,' in the nontechnical sense, when the various usages of the word have important meaning components in common. These different senses can be found, for example, under the same dictionary entry, while different meanings would be found under different entries—depending on the extent to which these meanings exclude one another.

Thus the three concepts of humiliation discussed here are not three separate meanings but merely three different senses with close links to one another. There is an especially close link between the senses of humiliation as rejection and as treating humans as nonhuman. The focus is different in each case, but the senses have many shared elements. When I speak of different concepts of humiliation, then, it should always be understood that I am referring to different senses rather than different meanings.

Humiliation in all its senses is especially closely linked to the negative justification for respecting humans, which involves the prohibition of humiliation as a type of cruelty that can be directed only at human beings. Taking away a creature's control by tying or locking it up is clearly also a manifestation of cruelty to animals, but what is unique to loss of control as a way of humiliating humans is not merely the cruelty of physical confinement but the symbolic element, which expresses the victim's subordination.

Cruelty is thus the mediating concept between the negative justification for respecting humans and the various elements of humiliation. The relation between cruelty and humiliation, however, is not simple. A decent society as a nonhumiliating society is not simply a special case of the principle that avoidance of cruelty must come first.[4] The complexity of the relation between cruelty and humiliation is illustrated by the following story about the indigenous tribes of North America. It is told that these tribes used to torture enemies they respected more cruelly than enemies they despised. The reason was that they wanted to give the enemies they respected a chance to demonstrate their stamina and restraint in the face of severe torture, thus enabling them to die a hero's death. They denied this opportunity to the enemies they despised, partly because they assumed that these despicable creatures would not be capable of dying as heroes.

I cannot vouch for the historical truth of this story, but the mere fact that we are able to understand it attests to the complexity of the relationship between cruelty and humiliation. In this story physical cruelty—the primary sense of cruelty—actually constitutes an expression of respect, while avoiding cruelty toward an enemy is intended as a humiliating act.

I therefore propose a distinction between a bridled society and a decent one. A bridled society avoids physical cruelty—it does not employ physical punishment, for example, or even backbreaking labor—but it does not avoid the institutional humiliation of its dependents. It is therefore not a decent society.

The question is whether the various types of society should be placed in lexicographical order, with the bridled society taking precedence over the decent one, which in turn precedes the just society. In other words, must we first establish a bridled society according to Judith Shklar's principle of "putting cruelty first," and only afterward seek to prevent humiliation; or should we avoid establishing an order of priorities among the types of society?

The relation between the bridled and the decent society—and here we must keep in mind that we are talking about ideal types of society—is intimately connected with our attitude to colonial regimes, which were often more restrained in their physical cruelty than the regimes they replaced. Nevertheless, the colonial regimes were usually more humiliating, and more rejecting of their subjects as human beings, than the local tyrants, who considered their subjects their fellow nationals or fellow tribe members and thus equal to them as human beings. If the principle of "putting cruelty first" means "First eradicate physical cruelty and only then eradicate mental cruelty," then matters are not simple, as is attested by the difficulty we have in deciding between the humiliating colonial regime that avoids physical cruelty and the physically cruel but nonhumiliating local tyranny. This difficulty of ours may attest that we are being forced to choose between two evils, and it is no wonder we find it hard to decide which is the lesser.

All other things being equal—which they definitely are not in the case of the two regimes in the above example— the eradication of physical cruelty comes first. Thus I advocate a lexicographical order of priorities in which the bridled society comes first, the decent society next, and the just society last. This order is cumulative—that is, the decent society must also be bridled and the just society must also be decent. The relation between the decent and the just society is discussed in the Conclusion.

I have already mentioned the tension between humiliation, on the one hand, and the skeptical justification based on the attitude of respect to humans, on the other. The bulk of the tension is concentrated in two of the senses of humiliation: treating humans as nonhuman and rejecting human beings from the "Family of Man." If humans are humiliated in either of these two ways, then how can the attitude of respect to humans be relied on as a basic given? I have already explained that the skeptical justification is based not on an antecedent fact of respect for human beings as human in practice, but rather on the concept of the attitude of respect that all human beings deserve. Indeed, it is precisely these two senses of humiliation that attest to the existence of a background concept of treating humans with respect, for in the absence of such a concept there could be no humiliation, at least not as an intentional act. In order for it to be conceptually possible to perceive the rejection of a human being from the Family of Man as an act of humiliation, there must be a background assumption of the basic respect due to human beings, such that deviating from it results in humiliation. Humiliation is a concept based on contrast, and the opposite of humiliation is the concept of respect for humans. If there is no concept of human dignity, then there is no concept of humiliation either.

9

Citizenship

Since a decent society involves respect for humans, and humiliating any human being is wrong, no distinction should be made in this regard between members of the society and people in its orbit who are not members. It is for this reason that I do not define the decent society as one that does not humiliate its members, but extend the concept to include anyone under its jurisdiction.

The notion of jurisdiction needs to be clarified. Dutch society, as a system including only its citizens in The Netherlands, was a decent society, or close to being so, at the time when the country was a colonial power. It was not a decent society, however, to the people it ruled in Indonesia, and it was therefore disqualified from being considered a decent society in general. Colonial societies must be judged not only by how their institutions treat their citizens at home but also by how they treat their subjects in the colonies.

When a society is an encompassing group, we may then ask how this society treats its members. This is a narrower question than the previous one, which asked how the society treats all its dependents, both members and nonmembers. The present question is what it means to belong to that society and how this belonging is reflected in the way the society's institutions treat its members. One very important question for determining if the society is a decent one is the question of whether it rejects the membership of those who are supposed to belong to it. The last question is not confined solely, or even primarily, to the issue of formal acceptance in the society, but refers to a broader sense of belonging to it.

A natural setting for discussing the issue of the decent society is the nation-state. On the whole, a nation-state fulfills the function of an encompassing group for its citizens. By restricting the discussion to nation-states I am not limiting its generality, since the principles we will be discussing can be extended to social settings that do not constitute nation-states.

My first claim is that a decent society does not injure the civic honor of those belonging to it. A more familiar version of this claim is that in a decent society there are no second-class citizens. In ancient Rome citizens enjoyed special public privileges, such as voting at assemblies, army service, the right to hold public office, and the legal right to sue and to defend themselves against suits. There were also private rights in Rome, such as the right to get married and to do business, but a crucial distinction was made between public and private rights. During a certain period the Romans offered the Latin nations they had conquered citizenship without public rights. Indeed, some of the battles between Rome and its neighbors in Italy were over the extent of the citizenship that should be granted to foreigners. The Roman notion of second-class citizenship meant citizenship without voting rights.

My reason for describing second-class citizenship in ancient Rome is that it highlights an important fact: second-class citizenship involves not only depriving people of essential resources and being unwilling to share authority but also the idea that second-class citizens are not in essence whole human beings—in other words, that they cannot become responsible adults. In this sense second-class citizens are rejected not only from full participation in the society but also from full participation in the "community of adults." The struggle to enfranchise women at the awakening of modern democracy involved the same sort of issue to a certain extent—namely, it was a struggle against the view of women as incomplete human beings.

Citizenship is typically a membership status involving rights. Second-class citizenship comes in two forms: denying the prevailing full citizenship rights to someone who is a citizen, and withholding citizenship from someone entitled to it.

The first type of second-class citizenship does not always involve formally denying people's rights. Sometimes there is discrimination in applying these rights—that is, recognized rights are not honored, and this occurs systematically. Second-class citizenship can also involve denying some rights to individuals who are recognized as citizens—rights that are granted in practice to other citizens.

The second type of second-class citizenship involves actually withholding formal citizenship in a state from individuals who are (morally) entitled to belong to that state. Instead, these individuals are given a different, inferior status, such as that of permanent residents. This is an inferior status from the point of view of people who want to join the society as citizens, although not necessarily for those who are merely taking refuge in the state without being interested in citizenship there.

Palestinian Arabs claim that they are second-class citizens in Kuwait, and Israeli Arabs maintain that they are second-class citizens in the state of Israel. These are two different claims. The claim regarding Kuwait is that Palestinians who were born in Kuwait, and have lived and worked there all their lives, are denied Kuwaiti citizenship even though they are entitled to it. The Israeli Arabs, in contrast, possess formal Israeli citizenship, but they are denied various civil rights, and others are not applied to them. The example of the Israeli Arabs is an interesting one. The majority of Israeli Arabs do not perceive Israel as an encompassing group that they need for their self-definition, and for some of them belonging to it is even quite embarrassing. Nevertheless, their insistence on equal civil rights is not merely a demand for just distribution of whatever goods and services are distributed to citizens, such as government housing mortgages on easy terms; the fact that they are denied these goods, even by a society they do not identify with, is perceived not only as injustice but also as humiliation.

Discrimination in the distribution of goods and services is a form of humiliation even if the people deprived of them do not define themselves as belonging to the depriving society. They may define themselves technically as members of the society—for example, for the purpose of getting a passport—but such membership is not a constitutive element of their self-definition. Nevertheless, they are humiliated by the fact that they are denied civic privileges. The humiliation comes from the sense that you do not want the discriminators to define you. You do not want to be a member of their society, yet you do not want them to say that you are not worthy of belonging to it. I believe that many Israeli Arabs feel this way.

What about minorities that enjoy rights which are not granted to the general public? For example, in China the right to have more than one child is granted to some minorities and withheld from the majority, but it would be quite ludicrous to see this right as a form of humiliation, since it is clear from the context that it is considered a privilege which is envied by the majority.

Nevertheless, we can imagine a culture in which the prevailing notion is that the proper family size is two children, and that a larger number of children makes the family into "animals." In a society with such a culture, not prohibiting the members of minorities from having more than two children could be interpreted as treating them like animals. A dog's "right" to urinate in public is not a privilege that is withheld from us humans.

Being rejected from an encompassing group may thus humiliate even those who do not want to be members of the group, but have the right to be. Moreover, even if what is being distributed is a burden, such as service in the Israeli army, those excluded (Israeli Arabs) may be relieved, but they are not necessarily happy about the fact that they are not being included (asked to serve). The claim I am advancing is that the problem of discrimination in civil rights is not only an issue of distributive justice but also a matter of humiliation: second-class citizenship of whatever form may be not only depriving but humiliating. Citizenship in a decent society must be egalitarian in order not to be humiliating. The feeling accompanying second-class citizenship is not just that of being a second-class citizen but also that of being a second-rate human being.

Aristotle thought that Man's defining trait is his being a political animal. According to Aristotle, the more we strip away Man's political characteristics the more animal he becomes. In other words, he is rejected from the human commonwealth. Taking away Man's political features means, in Aristotle's view, preventing him from being a citizen—that is, an active participant in the life of the polis. Aristotle distinguished between a good citizen and a good man. A good citizen is good as a citizen but not necessarily as a man. But a man who is not a citizen, according to Aristotle, is not a full-fledged human being—he is deprived of an essential human trait. I do not claim that being a political creature is a defining trait for adult humans, but I do accept the Aristotelian idea that second-class citizenship—whether in the form of withholding citizenship or of systematic discrimination in civil rights— may belong to the category of rejecting human beings as full-fledged humans and not only as citizens in a particular society.

One may counter that there is no point in defending the idea that a decent society is one in which there are no second-class citizens, and which has an egalitarian concept of citizenship. Children are citizens, but even in democratic states sensitive to children's rights no one claims that they ought to have the right to vote, for example, or to be elected to the society's institutions. Prisoners too are denied civil rights in a large number of states—for example, the right to vote in parliamentary elections—without this being a prima facie reason for disqualifying the state from being considered decent. To say that a state in which there is second-class citizenship cannot be considered a decent society is therefore too sweeping to be useful.

The argument against second-class citizenship based on considerations of human dignity is that such citizenship can be interpreted as tainting a person or a group with not being full-fledged human beings. On one interpretation, as nonadult human beings, this means that they are incapable of being responsible for their life as expressed in public decisions. But children are included in the category of nonadult human beings by definition. What prevents this from being humiliating is the fact that they are perceived as beings who will eventually grow up. Treating an adult as a child is patronizing, and treating an adult as a perpetual child is humiliating, but treating a child as a child is no humiliation. If a mother cannot accept the fact that her daughter is an adult and sees her as a perpetual child, is she humiliating her? Yes and no. Yes, because she does not accept the daughter as an adult who is responsible for her actions. No, because she accepts her as belonging to the family without qualification, and the principal motif in humiliation is rejection. (The issue of the rejection of prisoners will be discussed later, in Chapter 16.)

The Denial of Tripartite Citizenship

T. H. Marshall claims that the concept of citizenship can be divided into three layers: legal citizenship, political citizenship, and social citizenship.[1] Each aspect is characterized by a cluster of rights and privileges. Legal citizenship is the totality of rights that citizens have in matters involving the law. These include mainly rights connected with personal status. Political citizenship includes political rights as well, such as the right to vote in elections and the right to run for political office. Social citizenship includes citizens' rights to social benefits, such as health services, education, employment, and social security. Marshall claims that this tripartite division also fits the historical evolution of the concept of citizenship in nation-states. In the eighteenth century legal citizenship was stressed, through the idea of "equality before the law." In the nineteenth century it was political citizenship that was emphasized, with the slogan, "One man, one vote." In the twentieth century the demand for social citizenship has taken its place in the center of the political arena.

There is a familiar claim that citizenship which does not include a comprehensive social component is second-class citizenship. Members of classes lacking economic and social power are not full citizens even in the legal and political senses. They are not equal before the law, and their chances of being elected for political office are slim. The first two aspects of citizenship do not guarantee complete belonging in the society. The economic have-nots— especially the "underclass"—often manifest social alienation in forms ranging from indifference to hostility, even if these people are citizens in the formal sense.

There is another equally familiar claim that citizenship is a public good meant to be enjoyed by everyone. Adam Smith, the radical defender of the free market, thought that (vocational) education should be provided free to the working class, since only this could guarantee that their children would be able to join the society as full citizens. For him full citizens are productive citizens.

Even people opposed to taxation believe that it is necessary to make transfer payments to help turn second-class citizens into first-class citizens. The view of social citizenship as a public good has become an important argument in favor of the welfare state. Yet, true as it is, it is not my argument. My argument in favor of the third component of citizenship is not an instrumental one. If social citizenship includes, for instance, health services, then the justification for providing them, in my view, is not the fact that the ill may not be able to participate actively in the society, so that there is a general social interest in making them well. The proper justification is rather the fact that making ill people well is a good thing in itself. I expand on this and related issues in Chapter 14, where I deal with the question of the relation between the decent society and the welfare state. Here I want to add a few comments on the periphery of the problem of social citizenship. More specifically, I want to concentrate on matters pertaining to the symbolic aspect of social citizenship.

Symbolic Citizenship: The Fourth Dimension

I suggest a fourth aspect of the concept of citizenship: the aspect of symbolic citizenship—that is, sharing in the society's symbolic wealth. This component is generally not defined in terms of rights, and it is often mediated through the rights of a collective within the society. One example is the right of a minority group to have its language recognized as an official language of the state.

My claim is that a decent society is one that does not exclude any group of citizens from symbolic citizenship. It has no second-class citizens on the symbolic level.

The requirement of not excluding any citizen or group of citizens from the symbolic aspect of the state may be far-reaching, depending on the degree of stringency in one's interpretation of the word 'excluding.' If the society is not religiously homogeneous, this requirement can be fulfilled by separating religion from the state. Thus, for example, in a state such as Great Britain, it would be manifested by demanding that the head of state—the queen—should not serve as the head of the Anglican church. Many British citizens are not Anglican, and giving an Anglican aspect to a central symbol of the state— namely, the queen—would exclude these people from this symbolic level of the society, thus turning them into sec- ond-class citizens.

The requirement of not excluding any group from the symbolic realm is countered by the argument that one of the main purposes of the symbolic dimension of a soci- ety—in this case, the state—is to create a sense of loyalty through the identification of the citizens with the state. This requires evocative symbols with the power to affect people spiritually and emotionally. Such symbols cannot be produced synthetically and at will, but must be the product of an organic historical process. In the case of Britain, the connection between church and state evolved throughout history, and abolishing it would deprive the symbols of their power to stir people to action—for in- stance, the action required in war. Depletion of the sym- bols' power is liable to bring about a situation in which most British citizens would no longer be tied to their kingdom emotionally, which might in turn sap Britain's vitality.

Artificial attempts to dilute a country's symbols in order

to allow minorities to participate in them may weaken the majority's ability to identify with their country. In such an event there would not be much point in having a symbolic dimension in the society at all. Belonging to a country is not like joining an insurance company. Such a company may well have a trademark and jingle of its own, but a trademark is not a national symbol, and a jingle is not a national anthem. The question is how much it would cost to deprive citizens of the symbolic dimension of their national identification. The question becomes sharper in light of the reality that the symbols which draw the majority together and produce a sense of deep identification with the country are on many occasions directed against a minority group within the country. It seems that there is a great deal of truth in the clever remark that a nation is a collection of people who hate their neighbors and share a common illusion about their ethnic origin. When the hated neighbors are residents of the country, and the national symbols are directed against them, the problem raised by these symbols becomes exceedingly important.

When we say that some symbols are directed against a minority, we mean that the symbols are liable to make members of the minority feel actively rejected by the society. Whether this is a matter of humiliation or insult for the minority depends on the force and significance of the symbols. But as a first approximation the constraint on the society's symbolic treasury is that it should not contain symbols directed against a minority. A more difficult question is what should be done when the minority cannot share the symbols in the society's treasury because all of them are taken from the majority's history and culture. In such a case I suggest as a first approximation that this is a problem for the just society, since such a society requires the just distribution of the symbols in its treasury, but it is not a problem for the decent society.

The principle of symbolic citizenship in a decent society must be at least the following: a decent society must not develop or support on an institutional level any symbols that are directed explicitly or implicitly against some of the citizens of the state.

10

Culture

The question of what the culture of a decent society must be has an obvious answer: a culture that does not humiliate those in its orbit. But behind this obvious remark there are problems associated in part with the cultural and aesthetic price we may be willing to pay so that the culture does not humiliate anyone.

One may ask whether, in order to create a decent society, the spirit of cultural creativity must be restricted by an external norm, such as the one that says we should not humiliate others. Let's say Shylock and Fagin are literary figures that constitute a source of humiliation for Jews. Does this mean that a decent society must restrict the production or publication of *The Merchant of Venice* and *Oliver Twist*? Can we demand that a decent society interpret *The Merchant of Venice* positively, in a way that does not humiliate Jews but stresses the fact that Shylock in the play was a humiliated man who fought to defend his pride? Perhaps Jews have already acquired enough social confidence so that these works no longer seem humiliating to them. But what about more vulnerable minorities which are portrayed in the culture in humiliating ways?

The culture of a decent society must be a nonhumiliating one. This is an explicitly negative formulation. A decent society has no obligation to present anyone in a positive light, even vulnerable groups or individuals. In other words, the culture of a decent society does not require "socialist realism," where "the forces of progress" and vulnerable groups are portrayed in the best of lights.

But the question remains: Should we adopt a norm external to aesthetic creativity, such as a ban on humiliation, in order to secure the candidacy of our culture for the title of the culture of a decent society? Or should we rather protect cultural creativity from any sort of external intervention restricting the freedom of creation? Instead of asking what sort of culture is worthy of being considered the culture of a decent society, we are asking whether it is necessary or desirable to impose external norms on art. External norms are nonaesthetic norms. If we were willing to place restrictions on great art (high culture) in order to prevent humiliation, we could certainly make such a demand on lesser forms of art in a decent society, since the impositions of restrictions on such forms of art involves no serious artistic loss.

One possible reply to our question is to deny the claim that the requirement of nonhumiliation is a norm external to the work of art. Humiliating art is flawed art. Good art ought not to provide sound reasons for feeling humiliated. Art can be good in spite of the fact that it is humiliating, but this does not mean that its humiliating aspect does not diminish its aesthetic worth. Without a humiliating aspect, it would be even better. This response is worthy of study, but I do not want to channel the discussion toward issues of aesthetic appreciation and their connection with moral evaluation. For the purposes of this discussion I am assuming that nonhumiliation is an external criterion for appraising works of art. Obviously we must distinguish humiliating works from works that deal with humiliation and depravity, and even describe them with relish, such as the writings of the Marquis de Sade. De Sade's works should not humiliate us at all. In an anticlerical reading they can even uplift and refresh our souls.

The norm for art in a decent society declares that a work of art created or distributed in the society must not provide reasons for feeling humiliation. The counterargument, which states that great art even justifies humiliation, is a mistake. At best, the claim that the humiliating work of art is a great one can serve as a mitigating circumstance for the moral appraisal of the work. It mitigates our attitude to the work, but it does not abrogate the norm of nonhumiliation. A society whose works of art, whether good or bad, commit the sin of systematically humiliating individuals or groups is not a civilized society. And when this artistic humiliation is institutionally supported, for instance by subsidies, then the society is also not a decent one.

So far we have narrowed the question from the nature of culture in a decent society to a more specific question about the necessary constraints on high culture in such a society. The term "culture" is often used in the sense of "high culture." Its opposite is lack of culture or vulgarity. I do not want to restrict the concept of culture on elitist grounds, but I am equally averse to blurring the concept of high culture on populist grounds. Such blurring is based on the argument that the contrast between high and low culture is a class conflict rather than a cultural clash. In the populist view the distinction between the two types of cultures is a distinction without merit, reflecting only "class" bias. The concept of culture is a contested one, and I have no need here to enter into the controversies surrounding it.

We must first distinguish between cultural institutions and cultural contents. Cultural institutions include educational institutions such as schools, communication media such as newspapers and television, publishing houses, historical archives, museums, theaters, opera houses and the like. The contents of the culture include that which is created, preserved, transmitted, censored, forgotten, and remembered in the society and in the institutions that deal with these contents.

The basic question about the culture of a decent society must thus be divided into two. The first is: What should be the cultural contents of a decent society? What constraints, if any, must be placed on the contents of the culture so that they will be worthy of a decent society? The second question is: What constraints, if any, are to be imposed on the cultural institutions of a decent society? There is a close connection between these two questions: if, for example, plays in a decent society may not be humiliating—which relates to the contents of the culture—then the question with respect to the institutions is whether they must cut the subsidies given to a theater that puts on a humiliating play (such as Fassbinder's play, *Der Mull, die Stadt, und der Tod,* which was perceived as humiliating by Jews in Germany).

The distinction between cultural contents and cultural institutions can be challenged on the ground that it distorts the notion of culture. Culture is a matter not of content but of forms and possibilities of expression. Culture is an extension of the concept of language: it includes the entire system of symbols and signs available to a given society for its self-expression. Just as language is not characterized by its contents—it is characterized not by what is said with it but rather by what can be said—so too culture, being a system of symbols and signs and the possibilities of combining them, cannot and should not be contentually characterized. Culture is semiotic—that is, an extension of the concept of language to cover systems of signs and symbols in general.

The formal characterization of culture, I submit, is empty, since every natural language makes it possible in principle to "speak about everything," or almost everything. We should take symbols the way they are actually used rather than as a potential for expression in principle. Jewish society has had the means of expression for discussing not only the distinction between Jew and Gentile but even the contrast between Greek and barbarian. But while the former distinction was ready at hand and often used in Jewish discourse, the latter distinction played no role in it. Thus what interests us is not the question of what can be represented by the sign system of a culture, but what is actually represented—especially how people are represented, both as individuals and as groups. In British English there are many nasty idioms with reference to the Dutch: "Dutch comfort," meaning utterances such as "Soon things will be even worse"; "Dutch courage," meaning fake courage derived from alcoholic beverages; "Dutch widow," meaning a whore; and many other such expressions, all apparently deriving from the period of naval and trade rivalry between Britain and Holland. One may assume that the influence of these expressions on the way the British think about the Dutch today is minimal. Such expressions, however, might be activated to influence one's image of the "other." In any case, when we discuss symbols that define collective representations, we are referring to active symbols. Such symbols might very well be cliches—"tics" of our thinking—yet remain active.

We are interested in collective representation, which includes mainly symbols whose conceptual and emotional significance is shared by members of the society, and which are potent enough to contribute to identification with the group. An important role in collective representation is played by stereotypes of other social groups, some of which may exist within the society itself. A stereotype is not just a simplified, schematic representation of a group of people. Every form of classification or generalization is simplified and schematic, since simplifying and schematizing are a cognitive necessity. A stereotype is a particular kind of classification that gives disproportionately great weight to the negative characteristics of a group. It transforms features that are culturally and historically dependent into unchangeable inborn properties. It is for this reason that thinking based on stereotypes borders on racist thinking, in which innateness and permanence are attributed to traits that are acquired, temporary, and undesirable. Stereotypes, as a form of collective illusion, are wrong not because of their schematic simplicity, blurring individual differences, but because of the inordinate weight given to undesirable traits, rendered as innate.

The laziness of blacks, the excitability of Italians, the sneakiness of Armenians, the clannishness of Jews, the cruelty of Turks, the humorlessness of Germans—all these are negative traits, and attributing them to these groups is certainly insulting. But is it also humiliating?

To be sure, not all stereotypes are based on negative traits. There are many stereotypes based on positive traits, such as the blacks' sense of rhythm, the Italians' warmth, the Armenians' cleverness, the Jews' sense of family, the Turks' bravery, and the Germans' efficiency. My use of "stereotype" here refers only to negative ones, and my question, to repeat, is whether they are humiliating.

It seems that what is needed is a distinction between human stigmas and social stigmas. Human stigmas refer mainly to physical characteristics, and they disqualify their bearers from being, in some sense, part of humanity. Social stigmas are rather a matter of disqualifying or rejecting their bearers from being, in some sense, part of a particular society. Yet the two types of stigma are actually associated for people who have no society other than the rejecting one, such as Sicilians in Italy, Corsicans in France, and even Gypsies in various countries. These are people whose identity depends on the rejecting society, and who have no live option of choosing another society. For such people being rejected from their society, including being considered "second-class citizens," is tantamount to being rejected from humanity. Whether a social stigma or a stereotype is humiliating or merely insulting is not something that can be judged purely by the nature of the offensive trait that is attributed in the collective representation. What counts are the social consequences of such imputation, which cannot be guessed in advance.

Decency in Hegemonic Cultures

So far I have been using the concept of collective representation to mean a representation held in common by the members of a society, but the concept needs to be hedged. The problem of humiliating representation in cultures stands or falls with the hegemonic culture in the society. Only the hegemonic culture has the power to accept or reject people from the society as a whole. The concept of a hegemonic culture has two meanings. One meaning is that the culture of the dominant group in the society is the one with the power to decide who belongs to the society and who does not. In such a case there are cultures of other groups within the society that exist side by side with the hegemonic culture, but they are considered less important or even not considered at all. Another meaning of the concept is that there is one culture for the whole society, but this culture is determined by the dominant group, which also has control over it. The concept of collective representation as used here involves hegemonic culture in the second sense—namely, general culture shaped and controlled by the dominant group within the society.

I claim that a society is decent only if its hegemonic culture does not contain humiliating collective representations that are actively and systematically used by the society's institutions.

The immediate question that arises is: If culture in a decent society involves imposing restrictions on humiliating collective representations, wouldn't that turn the decent society into a puritanic one that doesn't let its members curse others, a society where purity of heart is taken to be purity of mouth? After all, the present-day secular version of this sort of puritanism is the "political correctness" movement, which permits only noninsulting "politically correct" expressions.

The risk in placing restrictions on humiliating styles of expression is the creation of a hypocritical society with an outward appearance of respectability whose members think derogatory thoughts that they refrain from expressing openly. The fear is that people in such a society are bound to express their nastiness indirectly. This might be worse than expressing it openly because it would be shrouded in respectability. If people are thinking humiliating thoughts about others it is better to let them vent these thoughts out in the open where they can be tackled. But even if we disregard the question of which is better—a society with a decent but hypocritical culture or one with a humiliating but nonhypocritical culture—we remain with the general question of whether it is right to impose constraints on means of expression in order to prevent humiliation.

I believe that the distinction here between a decent society and a civilized society is a distinction that makes a difference. (I consider this distinction identical with another important one, that between the absence of institutional discrimination—the decent society—and the absence of individual discrimination—the civilized society.) While it is important to be extremely wary of trying to constrain the way individuals express themselves, and the possibly humiliating or insulting way they use collective representations, it is not necessary to be so wary of restraining institutional expressions. In this category I include announcements by individuals speaking in the name of an institution. Such speakers include not only the institution's official spokespeople but all those with a role in the institution who can reasonably be taken as speaking in virtue of their role.

There may also be borderline cases where it is not clear whether speakers should be considered to be speaking in their own name or in the name of the institution. An interesting example of this sort, which arises out of the trend toward political correctness, is the status of remarks by university professors on campus. Should these be considered institutional expressions or individual expressions? On the one hand, the professors are speaking as teachers in an institutional setting, and should therefore be confined by the restrictions on institutions; on the other, this particular institutional setting is supposed to provide them with extended freedom of expression—namely, academic freedom. In any case, academic freedom is understood to mean that professors should enjoy at least the rights of expression of any individuals in the society. Thus, even though they hold institutional positions as teachers in an academic institution, they should be considered as individuals rather than as people speaking in the name of the institution.

Let us return to the distinction between the function of humiliating collective representations as used by individuals and as used by public institutions. As a rule, institutional humiliation, being rejection from an encompassing group by a social institution, is more harmful than humiliation by an individual in the society. Restricting the expression of individuals, however, is more damaging than restricting institutional expression. It is not difficult to see why this should be so. First of all, the element of threat to the victim of institutional humiliation is generally greater than in humiliation by a private individual, since institutions are generally more powerful than individuals and so can be more damaging. With regard to the humiliation itself, institutional humiliation involves rejecting the person from an encompassing group and is therefore perceived as rejection by the society as a whole, while in general this is not the case with humiliation by an individual. At the same time, restricting institutions' freedom of expression is not as bad as curbing individual freedom of expression, since the ultimate justification for freedom of expression is the well-being of the individual. Freedom of expression for institutions is parasitic on freedom of expression for individuals. If these considerations are correct, then it is reasonable to require that a distinction be made between restricting humiliating behavior on the individual and the institutional levels. Other things being equal, restrictions on institutions are more justified than restrictions on individuals.

An important test for the culture of a decent society is the case of pornography. A major if not constitutive element of pornography is the humiliating representation of women. Pornography does not represent sex—it arouses it. A by-product of this fact is that it represents women in a particularly humiliating way—namely, as merely a means for arousing men. Here again the distinction between a civilized and a decent society is critical. There is a difference between institutional uses of pornography, such as its distribution by the army as material for raising morale, and individual uses. Here too the restrictions on institutional pornography must differ from those on individual pornography. As a first approximation, it is right to restrict institutional pornography in order to keep one's society decent, but it is wrong to restrict pornography for individual use in cases where the participants are consenting adults.

Presence of Subgroups

Imagine a society which includes as a subgroup an encompassing group with its own form of life. The cultural institutions of the larger society, especially the media, do not, as a rule, provide public presence for the subgroup or its form of life. Although there are no degrading or even insulting collective representations of the encompassing subgroup in the media of the larger society, the subgroup and its form of life are ignored. Let's assume that this disregard is intentional, and that the subgroup's lack of public presence in the culture is the result of internal or external censorship. One could imagine, for example, that this is the situation of the gay community in certain societies, where it has become an encompassing group yet there is a deliberate attempt to ignore it. The society attempts to keep the gay community away from the public eye by isolating gays in closed clubs, bars, private parties, and the like. Should such deliberate disregard humiliate the encompassing group? Should disregard in general, whether intentional or not, be considered humiliating?

In order to simplify the discussion we will assume that there is no economic price for giving the encompassing subgroup public presence in the culture, and that there may even be a price for isolating them, in the form of loss of income (for example, there are no ads targeted at the subgroup, which might increase the number of sales within that community).

Deliberate disregard means denouncing and disqualifying the subgroup's form of life. But does this denunciation constitute humiliation? The encompassing group—in this example, the gay community—is right in seeing the society's intentional disregard of it as a judgment that its form of life lacks human value. The gays are justified in concluding that they are being denied the legitimacy of expressing themselves as human beings by presenting their form of life in public. Deliberate disregard of a worthwhile form of life provides the victims with a justification for considering this disregard a humiliating omission.

Not all forms of life possess human value, even if they bring great satisfaction to those who practice them. Forms of life that lack value are those in which humiliation is a constitutive element. Racist groups such as the Ku Klux Klan or the skinheads might constitute encompassing groups for their members, but they lack human value because their form of life is based essentially on humiliating others.

Ignoring a valueless group may provide its members with a reason to feel humiliated, but it is not a good reason. The question confronting us is not whether such groups ought to be represented in the culture of a decent society, but whether they should be allowed to exist at all in such a society. The answer to this question depends on the extent of the threat they pose to their victims. If they are allowed to exist, then the next question is whether such groups should be given public presence in the culture. They should not. The reason is that these groups have no value—or, more precisely, they have negative value. Lack of value and negative value are reasons to cancel the obligation (if there is one) to provide groups with a platform.

Should a decent society permit those who have been humiliated to react by humiliating those who have wronged them? In other words, is humiliation a legitimate form of protest in a decent society? The assumption is that the society is decent but not necessarily civilized. That is, we assume that there is no institutional humiliation, but that individuals or groups may be degraded in the society by other individuals or groups. Should a decent society allow the humiliated to organize themselves for the purpose of humiliating in return the evildoers and their accomplices who have wronged them? I am not referring to "Anti-Defamation Leagues" which reveal acts of defamation and humiliation against a victimized minority and denounce them in public, but to organizations using the weapon of humiliation to get society to pay attention to their plight. The question is not about a sort of "self-defense," responding to spitting by spitting back. The question is whether groups should be permitted to organize themselves for the purpose of humiliating other groups as an anti-establishment protest act—for example, in organized racist rap bands. In other words, can the existence of humiliating institutions of deprived or humiliated groups be compatible with the characterization of the decent society as a nonhumiliating society? Does the fact that they are nonestablishment institutions exempt them from being included among the institutions according to which we judge whether a society is a decent one? The question is not whether humiliation as an institutional act of revenge is an appropriate or efficient sort of response, but only whether it disqualifies a society from being a decent one. The case I am describing is the following: an anti-establishment subgroup uses its institutions to humiliate people who have deliberately degraded a minority group—say, organized Turks shaving the heads of neo-Nazis in Germany. The institutions of the larger society to which this group belongs refrain from performing humiliating acts, but there are acts of humiliation performed by individuals that are directed against the minority group. In such a case, is the society a decent one?

The type of case I am describing here is a borderline one for characterizing the decent society, because the institutions in question cannot be seriously considered the society's institutions, although they are institutions within the society. But since we have extended the institutional framework of the society to include not only basic institutions but also more peripheral ones, such as theaters, it would be somewhat odd for us to exclude groups such as immigrants' organizations from the totality of the society's institutions, even though they are organizations of marginal groups within the society. Thus my answer to the question is a conceptual postulation that the case I have described here disqualifies such a society from being considered decent.

Cultural Tolerance

Is a decent society a pluralistic society in principle? Of course, a decent society may in fact be homogeneous, in the sense that it evolved historically as a homogeneous society that does not contain any competing subgroups which constitute encompassing groups. Norway may be an example of such a society. But must any society—even a homogeneous one—in principle (by law, for example) permit the existence of competing legitimate encompassing subgroups in order to be considered a decent society? Forbidding legitimate encompassing groups to exist is humiliating to those wishing to form such groups, and so it might seem that a decent society must be pluralistic. There is, however, an alternative to a pluralistic society—namely, a tolerant society. The difference between them is that while a tolerant society acquiesces to competing ways of life, it does not see any value in such diversity. A pluralistic society, in contrast, not only tolerates competing ways of life but considers their very existence an important value. For a tolerant society, tolerance is the price which must be paid, and which is worth paying, to avoid the human suffering that a long history of the repression of competing forms of life has taught us is the inevitable result of intolerance. A tolerant society is thus tolerant for reasons of prudence, not principle. We have learned the most about the need for tolerance from the history of religious wars. This history has taught many European societies the bitter lesson that religious wars exact a heavy price. Thus religious tolerance is needed as a form of compromise with reality. It does not involve the acknowledgment that the competing group's form of life has value for the society as a whole.

An encompassing group is a competing group in the sense that anyone belonging to it cannot in principle belong to another encompassing group of the same type—for example, one cannot be both Catholic and Muslim. This is not merely a practical impossibility, such as the impossibility of living in the city and in the country at the same time. The principled impossibility of belonging to two encompassing groups of the same type means that there is an explicit or implicit command in the form of life of one group that prohibits belonging to the other. The Russian Narodniks (a socialist movement of the 1870s advocating a rural life) considered the urban and rural forms of life as competing encompassing groups, but in general they are not perceived in this way.

Pluralism is a stand from which value is assigned to competing forms of life. As a member of a pluralistic society who belongs to one side of the divide, I can acknowledge the value of a competing form of life, even if it is not a form of life that I would care to adopt for myself or wish my children to adopt. It is important to distinguish between competing and merely incompatible forms of life, although incompatible forms of life may easily exist in homogeneous societies as well. Being urban and being a farmer are incompatible forms of life, but they are not competing. Being religious and being secular are not only incompatible but competing as well. Forms of life are incompatible if it is technically impossible to live them both simultaneously. Forms of life are competing if they contradict one another, in the sense that the beliefs and values of each one contradict those of the others. Secular and religious forms of life are contradictory, not merely technically incompatible.[1] Pluralism does not mean that one cannot criticize other forms of life. One's criticism, however, must not constitute social or human rejection; on the contrary, one must recognize the human value of the competing forms of life not only for their members, but for everyone. I return to the difference between criticism and rejection in the next section.

The opening question of whether a decent society must be pluralistic can thus be understood as follows: Is it enough for the society to be tolerant, or must it also be pluralistic in order to be considered a decent society?

A tolerant society, properly understood, is sufficient to guarantee nonhumiliating institutions in the society. In other words, tolerance is sufficient for making the society a decent one. It is not necessary for this purpose that the society should be pluralistic as well. It is not clear, however, whether tolerance is enough to guarantee a civilized society. On the level of the relations among the members of the society, tolerance may not be sufficient. It depends on the nature of the tolerance. It could be, for example, the result of indifference. You see yourself as belonging to a given form of life. You are aware of the existence of a competing form of life, but you do not ascribe any value to it. It would be better, you say to yourself, if the adherents of that form of life would adopt ours, but you do not care enough to get excited about it. You are simply uninterested in the other form of life and its adherents. In short, you are indifferent to them. Your attitude has no emotion behind it: "If that's what they want, then let them live that way."

But there's also another sort of tolerance—a stance of social tolerance which recognizes the fact that the society's institutions must be tolerant, yet permits the existence of active hostility toward other forms of life on the personal level. These other forms of life may be considered not merely in error but actually sinful. Such a society is possible, and it would even be a decent one according to the present interpretation of this concept, but it would be a suspect society. This is because of the danger that the people holding positions in the society's institutions, who have this sort of hostile attitude toward competing forms of life, might express their humiliating attitude while performing their institutional tasks. In other words, the abstract attitude of the society's institutions, as encoded in their rules, might be a decent one, and all legitimate forms of life would be tolerated, but in the practical behavior of the representatives of these institutions the tolerance would be liable to disappear.

Criticism versus Rejection

A decent society is based on the principle that it may include encompassing groups which have competing and not merely incompatible forms of life.

An essential component of a form of life may be its denial of other forms of life. A secular form of life essentially denies a religious one, and all the more so vice versa. The question is when such denial is merely severe criticism and when it is humiliating rejection. Secularists may recognize the value of a religious form of life, believing that it contributes significantly to moral life, family life, community responsibility, the ability to withstand crisis situations, and the like. At the same time, they disagree with the historical and metaphysical beliefs which they attribute to the religious form of life, especially what it considers to be the source of authority in the conduct of one's life. Moreover, they may think it is based on superstition, prejudice, and wishful thinking. Such people see themselves as having a critical stance, even a radically critical stance, toward the religious way of life, but they do not usually consider their position as intended to be humiliating. However, they are probably not seen in the same way by those on the other side of the fence. For people belonging to the religious form of life, secularists are seen not as critics but as blasphemers. And if the secularists use the weapon of ridiculing satire, it is a safe bet that the victims of such satire see themselves as being presented in a degrading manner that arouses derision and detestation. What is criticism for the one may count as humiliation for the other.

Pluralistic societies, which encourage competing forms of life, are most likely to be in a state of tension between criticism and rejection. A vulnerable group with a history of humiliations and suspicion of its surroundings, especially suspicion of the dominant culture, is liable to interpret any criticism as humiliation. The hegemonic form of life may well be indifferent to such a peripheral form of life, so that it has no intention of criticizing it because it does not perceive it as a threat. The dominant culture may even consider the other culture too marginal to be worth criticizing. But such disregard is liable to be interpreted by an overly sensitive, vulnerable group as insulting. The marginal group may even be obsessed with the idea that the dominant group never stops thinking about it, and that its disregard is deliberate rather than the outcome of indifference. All this belongs to the bitter psychology of encompassing subgroups which were hurt in the past and so are overly sensitive in the present.

But then who decides what is permissible criticism and what is objectionable humiliation? One principle seems to suggest itself. Criticism is whatever you are willing to offer others and would be willing to accept if something similar were offered to you. Humiliation is whatever you express toward the other that you would consider humiliating if something analogous were directed at you. But in the case of vulnerable groups, the suggested principle is like telling a featherweight to take part in a boxing match with a heavyweight, with the argument that the heavyweight is willing not only to throw punches at his opponent but to take counterblows as well. Vulnerable groups in a society are often "featherweights" in this sense. Blows dealt by the socially "heavyweight" group are liable to knock them onto the floorboards, and even to end in a knockout rejecting them from the society as a whole.

At the same time, the principle that the vulnerable minority group should be allowed to decide what is humiliating is highly questionable. I have already given hints as to why this is so. Minority groups with a history of persecution often suffer from a cultural paranoia of humiliation and insult. They "fish" for insults in places where insults and humiliation cannot be seen by the unaided eye, even by an outside observer sympathetic to the minority group. The raw nerves of the group are liable to be so sensitive that even a compliment will be taken by it as an insult. A compliment extended in an atmosphere of cultural suspicion is taken as a sign of a condescending, patronizing attitude.

In contrast to the last observation, there is a counterobservation claiming that groups with a history of persecution and humiliation develop a thick skin for humiliation. There is some truth in both observations. Groups with such a history are liable to react in one of these two ways, or perhaps even in both ways at once, with a jumpiness affected by changing moods. The question is whether we can leave the decision about what counts as humiliation in the hands of a vulnerable group given to this sort of mood swing. I maintain that there must be a presumption in a decent society in favor of the interpretation given by vulnerable minorities as to the humiliating nature of the gestures directed at them. This presumption could be rebutted, for example, by showing that in the general context the humiliating interpretation is implausible. The justification for preferring that the society's presumption be in favor of the vulnerable group's interpretation is anchored in the moral necessity for tipping the balance of error in interpretation toward the side of the weak.

Let me explain. When we hold a presumption of innocence, for example, as in the saying "A person is innocent until proven guilty," we do not justify this presumption with a statistical demonstration that most of the people brought before a court are actually innocent. Most probably this is not so. The justification is a moral one, and its purpose is to regulate the court's errors in favor of the innocent. This purpose is expressed in such sayings as "It is better to let five criminals go free than to put one innocent person into prison." We have a preference as to which way the errors should go. An error leading to the punishment of an innocent person seems worse to us than an error enabling a guilty person to go free. Analogously, the justification for the presumption in favor of the vulnerable group's interpretation is that the errors ought to be balanced in its favor. Therefore the group's interpretation should be accepted unless and until it has been rebutted.[2]

A few years ago, at the University of Pennsylvania, a white student shouted the epithet "water buffalo" at a black woman in a group of black sorority members who were making noise outside a dorm late at night. This incident became a big issue because the woman and her friends interpreted the epithet as a racist remark, although the white student vehemently denied having had any racist intentions when he said it. One of the arguments put forward was that the remark was a racist one because the water buffalo is of African origin and has a black skin. (The water buffalo is actually brown and of Asian origin, but who knows that anyway?) The university's lawyer argued that the interpretation of a remark must be left to the person to whom it is made, so that the racist interpretation was the one that had to be accepted. This is not the position I am advocating here. What I argue is only that there is a presumption in favor of the black student's interpretation.

The charity principle in favor of the vulnerable group's interpretation must be offset by another principle: whatever would be considered criticism rather than humiliation if it took place "in the family," that is, within the group, must also be considered as such if it comes from outside the group. There are undoubtedly differences in context and intention between what occurs within the group and what may come from the outside, even if exactly the same expressions are involved. What is said as humorous criticism within the group, in a tone of forgiving self-ridicule, can be a manifestation of pure humiliation when coming from the outside, even if the expressions have the same content. Nevertheless, we must hold to the principle that society has no right to discriminate between the sides and determine that something should be considered criticism if it comes from within but humiliation if it comes from the outside. Once criticism, always criticism.

If my discussion has created the impression that humiliation is a purely verbal matter, it should be corrected. It is in order to avoid this that I have been using the term "expression," which can denote nonverbal expressions as well as verbal ones. After all, nonverbal expressions are frequently used for purposes of humiliation. The Nazi salute directed against immigrants in Berlin these days is harsher than words, as is the desecration of gravestones with swastikas.

But this is not enough. The culture of a decent society must include not only all the means of expression at the society's disposal but also its material culture—what is called civilization, as opposed to culture, in the romantic dichotomy. The purpose for which we are discussing culture includes material culture as well. The question of what the material culture of a decent society ought to be like is an important one. The technology available to a society is a significant factor in determining what is considered humiliating in that society. I am not only referring to status symbols connected with objects, such as cars of certain models and not others. Artifacts do indeed serve as communicative acts that can signal who belongs and who does not, through the use of what is "in" and what is "out." But beyond the communicative aspect of the culture, there is another concept of humiliation as the lack of the sort of control specifically relevant to technological civilization. As a paradigmatic example, consider the provisions made for handicapped people. In some societies considerable care is taken to provide special arrangements for the handicapped, thus giving them a large degree of independence. In other societies handicapped people are continually humiliated by the fact that they are dependent on the good will of others. This sometimes occurs despite the existence of the material means that could guarantee the handicapped a measure of independence. When a society can afford these means, but makes no effort to put them at the disposal of its handicapped, it humiliates them.

The special parking tags allocated to the handicapped are not a stigma. They should be considered not signs of humiliation but rather signs of benefit, since the tags that allow the handicapped to park in places prohibited to others are meant to increase their ability to control their movements and thus their lives. The allocation of these tags is therefore enhancing rather than humiliating. It is not the mere singling out of a group or a person that is humiliating, but only singling out for the purpose of distancing and suppressing people (as in the case of the yellow star). Parking tags for the handicapped are desirable because they are intended to achieve the opposite purpose.

IV

Putting Social Institutions
to the Test

11

Snobbery

Can a snobbish society be a decent one? There is a simple answer: if the snobbish society is humiliating, then it is not a decent one; but if it is not humiliating, then it can be considered a decent society. This answer, however, is not very helpful. What we want to know is whether a snobbish society is essentially a humiliating one—more precisely, whether there is a conceptual connection between snobbery and humiliation. We tend to forgive snobbery as a familiar and almost amiable peccadillo, the stuff that furnishes English comedies in which gaunt old ladies hold bone china teacups and mutter nasty remarks about an embarrassed, ambitious young man who happens to be "too common." Not terribly nice but not really terrible either. Since snobbery is based on faux pas connected with trivial social cues, we are inclined to consider the entire phenomenon a trivial one. But a sequence of trivial steps can lead to a nontrivial outcome, and so it is with snobbery. Evelyn Waugh typifies the menace of snobbery—the sophisticated, mocking, wicked snob, not the pathetic, absurd snob of English comedy.

The problem for our purposes is institutional snobbery.

There is a question about the exact nature of the problem: Is it a problem of humiliation, or merely a matter of embarrassment? I take embarrassment quite seriously. Many people have taken crucial steps in their lives solely in order to avoid embarrassment. Sinclair Lewis's Babbitt married a woman solely because it would have been embarrassing for him to refuse her. Still, embarrassment is not humiliation, and one may deliberately embarrass others without humiliating them. What one does is create a vexing situation in which the bewildered others have an acute sense of not knowing what to do. Embarrassment may diminish self-esteem, but should not affect self-respect. So the question is whether snobbery is based merely on embarrassing those who do not belong, or whether it also humiliates them. Snobbery is liable to serve as a sort of cartel for allocating honors in a society which may not be just, yet is not humiliating either. Thus the question of what is wrong with snobbery in the present context is not the general question of the sins of snobbery and snobs. There are many things wrong with them.[1] Our question is more focused: Is snobbery humiliating?

Snobbery involves big names—associating oneself with big names and dissociating oneself from the nameless. With impressive achievements one can make a name for oneself, but it is even better to be born to it. A snobbish society is one that may turn the achievement orientation of society into a belonging orientation. Snobbery is based on a continual elaboration of the signs of belonging to the ingroup so that the "others" will always be excluded from the society that counts. Signs of belonging are acquired by direct acquaintance, not by remote description. This is what makes it so difficult for outsiders to penetrate the society if they are not in the orbit of its tone-setters. Impressive achievements may penetrate the armor of the snobbish society. It is not achievements that are the name of the game, however, but the name that is made by these achievements. Outsiders who have not mastered the signs of belonging behave awkwardly and embarrassingly—embarrassing themselves most of all. They are relentlessly tripped up by insiders placing stumbling blocks in their path, so that it becomes difficult for them to make their way into the society. This nasty twist on "Chutes and Ladders," where outsiders are supplied with more chutes than ladders, is not innocuous, and it can be very harmful indeed.

Institutional snobbery may be expressed, for example, in prestigious clubs which can be entered only according to special codes, as well as in fancy invitations to glittering institutional affairs. Those with hopes of joining such places are bound to find themselves insulted and embarrassed by not being included among the invitees, or at least not among the invitees that count. But all these are social games with social honor as their payoff. They can exclude you from the in-group but they cannot reject you from the human commonwealth. A snobbish society may nevertheless set the tone for total rejection when the society as a whole behaves that way. In short, an ordinary snobbish society is not humiliating in and of itself, but within the general social and cultural context it can definitely foster and encourage humiliation that is not only personal but institutional as well.

Let us now consider an opposite argument, which may shed light on the historical and social role of the snobbish society, and on the development of the concepts of respect and humiliation so central to the concept of the decent society. Here I argue in favor of snobbery, or at least defend it, as a necessity that should not be condemned.

Norbert Ellis claimed that modern man was formed by a sequence of tiny changes that accumulated over time into one significant change.[2] These incremental changes involve the concepts of fastidiousness and shame, and they have become critical since the Renaissance. They are manifested in eating and drinking habits, in clothing and hair styles, and especially in strict control over the body and its secretions. Some of these changes were manifested in the creation of intimate spaces—bedrooms, toilets, bathrooms. These changes shaped the conception of the private self, which we seek to protect from humiliation. Each of these steps in the process of change seems trivial, but the cumulative results are far-reaching. During the Middle Ages people spat on the floor, later they stamped on the spit with their foot, later still they began using a spittoon, and finally nowadays all spitting in public is frowned upon. Anyone caught in the act of spitting is liable to feel ashamed and embarrassed in civilized society. Similarly, people used to wipe their nose on their sleeve, then with their left hand, then with just two fingers, and finally with a handkerchief. Each such step is a small one, but the end result is control over the body's secretions, as a prelude to the creation of separate public and private spaces. It was not the bourgeois who created the mores of control over the body as a prelude to "capitalist control" over it. The source of these mores was the snobbish royal courts—along with their annexes, the homes of the nobility—while the upper-middle class, which was trying to join high society, carefully imitated its manners. The lower-middle class was the next to copy these manners, and finally they trickled down to those members of the working class who were interested in upward mobility. The social function of these manners has always been to create class distinctions.

There is no need to make sophisticated assumptions about "latent functions." The issue is clear, and can be illustrated by the history of eating with a fork. Etiquette was invented to distinguish between people and has created barriers between people. Yet it has also created the concept of social space and the borders within which the private individual is located. Nobles were not embarrassed to be seen naked in their bedroom by their servants because the servants' eyes did not count, whereas today we are embarrassed if a stranger catches sight of our unmade bed. The bedroom has turned into the private temple of the individual. Partitioning space into public and private sectors, like partitioning the body into zones that can be revealed and those that must remain covered, is of the highest importance in creating the concept of the private individual through the notion of privacy. Not all this was said by Ellis, but it is all in the spirit of the claim inspired by him. Manners are the tools of the snob. Snobs raise etiquette to the level of ethics. The purpose of manners, as mentioned, is to exclude people from fastidious, worthy society. But even if this is their purpose and the snob is aware of it, the historical outcome is a decisive contribution to the development of the concept of privacy, which has led to the concept of the private individual. And, after all, these concepts form the basis of the modern notion of dignity as well as the modern notion of humiliation.

Fastidious manners are indeed a well-known instrument of snobs, but it is not their only one. The snobbish-ness of "old-timers" may be manifested instead in rough, familiar manners that are likewise intended to keep away strangers, who, as newcomers, cannot allow themselves the rough and hearty familiarity of the old-timers.

The conceptual importance of this last argument lies partly in the fact that it points to the fallacy of composition with regard to the concept of the trivial. The introduction of each new form of manners is trivial and arbitrary in and of itself. Yet the cumulative social change resulting from a sequence of such steps is of far-reaching conse-quence. Even in mathematics, every complete proof con-sists of steps each of which is based on only one rule of deduction and so is trivial, yet the entire proof may be quite profound. As I have said, we must not be misled by the triviality of the concerns on which a snobbish society is based into devaluing the importance of creating a social foundation for developing the modern concepts of private and public, of honor and humiliation. But to return to our main concern, even if we accept Ellis's historical de-scription, it cannot serve to justify a present-day snobbish society as a society of formal manners with the purpose of social exclusion. Even if such a society was once vital for the development of the concept of a decent society, it is no longer necessary.

Fraternity

The silent partner in the trinity of liberty, equality, frater-nity is the last one. The difficulty in explicating the term fraternity, and turning it into a social ideal in its own right, is to a great extent an outcome of the fact that fraternity is part of the background of the other two values, since it is the human bond on which society is based, but it itself has no clear background. The model for fraternal relations, as the name attests, is the relationship between siblings. This is a connection of unconditional belonging. The difficulty lies, of course, in the idea that an anonymous society of the masses could be based on such a family bond. Skepticism about fraternity is like skepticism about Emerson's vision that all humanity might be lovers of one another.

The idea of encompassing groups assumes that there is a human possibility of feeling a sense of fraternity even toward unfamiliar people, if they can be identified as belonging to the encompassing group. Jews see themselves as belonging to an extended family. The socialists of the First Internationale believed that solidarity among workers who shared a common fate would be stronger than the sense of belonging to other encompassing groups, such as religion or nationality, if they could only succeed in forming a class consciousness among the workers. But the idea of fraternity also has the vulgar version of student fraternities. This is not the camaraderie of combat soldiers sharing a common fate, but the fraternity of pals having a good time together. Such comradeship can provide warmth and closeness, but it is often mixed with humiliating treatment of those who do not yet belong, frequently taking the form of tormenting initiation rites as the price of joining the fraternity.

It is an interesting fact that many initiation rites include humiliating elements. This is the case with new boarders at public schools, raw recruits in elite army units, new students in fraternities, and the like. The humiliation in these instances is directed not against people with a marginal status in the society but against people with a liminal status—that is, people in a transition stage between two social categories, on the way up in the social hierarchy. The meaning of these humiliating rites is that you are not worthy of the fraternity you are joining until you have passed excruciating initiation trials.

Is there place in a decent society for displays of humiliation in its (prestigious) institutions, as part of their initiation rites? Is, for example, the degradation of recruits in voluntary elite army units the same as a debasing sadomasochistic relationship between consenting adults, which we have not excluded from the decent society? It is true that humiliating liminal individuals is different from rejecting marginal persons, mainly because humiliating the liminal is a temporary phenomenon restricted to the initiation. Still, at the time it is taking place it is a wretched form of humiliation; moreover, it is humiliation with an institutional touch. It is institutional humiliation not in the sense of being done in the name of a social institution, but in the sense of occurring systematically within such institutions. Humiliating bonds between sadomasochistic individuals are an issue for a civilized society, but here we are dealing with cases in which institutions are vicariously involved. A decent society is incompatible with liminal humiliation even if it is taken as a temporary menace en route to great fraternity. Humiliation is humiliation, and fraternity should not be attained at the price of it.

Bodily Signs

Bodily signs play a most important part in people's identity and in their identification with encompassing groups.

It is not difficult to understand why humiliation is often directed at bodily features and clothing. This is an attack on important components of the identity of one's personality. One's type of hair, the structure of one's nose and cheekbones, and the shape of one's eyes can all serve as a source of pride or shame. Humiliation often takes the form of insulting gestures directed at bodily signs, as well as items of clothing perceived as "natural extensions" of the body.

Snobbish and vulgar societies each have their own particular reactions to bodily features and clothing. If the army demands that its recruits have uniform crewcuts, while a particular recruit's form of life includes long hair, there is a clash between the two lifestyles, and the institutional demand for a haircut may be interpreted not only as coercion but also as humiliation. If someone whose religion has a clear rule against haircuts—a Sikh soldier, for example—is required to cut his hair, he will interpret this as an act of degradation. But if a young man belongs to a rock group or a rock culture in which long hair has social significance, is he too justified in considering himself humiliated in the face of army rules demanding that he cut his hair? One may assume that the rock fan's shorn locks will bring hearty catcalls from his pals, ridiculing the recruit when he is on leave. Yet the demand for a haircut is not itself humiliating. Still, a rock or leftist lifestyle can signify a nonbourgeois form of life, with long hair as its bodily representation. The German army, for example, recognized during the sixties that such lifestyles are worthy of respect; recruits were no longer ordered to cut their hair.

The way a decent society ought to treat the identifying bodily signs of a legitimate form of life depends on the meaning given within that form of life to the identifying mark. The society whose institutions we are examining may even have its own interest in its members' bodily signs, an interest that may well clash directly with the forms of life of encompassing groups within the society. The dominant culture, which shapes the behavior of the society's basic institutions, may be interested, for example, in displaying bodily signs of "modernity," order and efficiency. Peter the Great had the beards of the Boyars shaved off in order to demonstrate that Russia was cutting itself off from its tradition and entering the new Western era. Kemal Ataturk acted similarly with respect to traditional dress, requiring his officials to wear European attire. The story of the Muslim girl in the Parisian suburb who came to school in a traditional headgear brought this contrast into dramatic prominence. Her dress conflicted with that customary in her school, and not only was it perceived as a challenge to the dominant form of life, but the religious context of the girl's attire was perceived as an attempt to resist the separation of religion from the educational system.

There is a new, noteworthy element in our discussion of bodily signs. The context of the discussion of tolerant or pluralistic societies was the competition between encompassing groups with rival forms of life. The competition involved in the present discussion, however, is between the society as a whole and subgroups within it. The question is whether the new context requires a new principle. One stricture is that the question itself is based on a mistake. The assumption that the society as a whole is confronting a minority group within itself is misleading. The contestants are not the society as a whole versus a minority group, but the dominant group in the society, which aspires to speak for the society as a whole, versus a minority group within the society.

Irrespective of the proper description of the clash, the principle of tolerance should serve us in the present context as well, especially when we are specifically considering the body and its clothing. The army is an exception on this issue. The reason for this claim of mine is functional. Army discipline requires a great deal of uniformity in its lifestyle. There is thus a substantive justification for such uniformity, and resisting it requires a weighty reason, such as possible harm to freedom of religion, as in the case of the Sikh's long hair. This is not the case with the long hair of rock culture. The difference between the two lies in the fact that in rock culture the commitment to a specific hairstyle is a question of fashion, not of principle. Today long, tomorrow short. Hair (or the lack of it) is important to rock culture, but the particular style can change. In religious settings, in contrast, there is an obligation to wear one's hair in a specific unchanging way, with sanctions imposed on anyone who changes this hairstyle.

The justification for the exception granted to the army is purely functional. The symbolic function of military appearance as a symbol of identity and identification is not immune to counterclaims of those who prefer other forms of life. In other words, choosing a military appearance for nonfunctional reasons of symbolizing social uniformity is the act of a militaristic society. Thus when the arena is shifted from the army to the school, uniformity is no longer functionally justified, as it is in the army. There is no justification for imposing quasi-military bodily signs in schools. In the case of schools nothing stands in the way of the tolerance principle. According to my understanding of the tolerance principle guiding the decent society, such a society must accept the request of that Muslim girl in Paris to wear her traditional dress in school.

There is, however, one reservation that should be made in reference to this case. It applies to the situation where the school has a uniform dress code, which is intended as a valuable means of creating equality among the pupils and blurring distinctions of class and origin. It is generally the children of immigrants who are the main beneficiaries of the uniform dress code. In the case where the school does not have such a code, however, the restriction on the Muslim girl is unjustified.

12

Privacy

The institutions in a decent society must not encroach upon personal privacy. There is a close connection between encroachment upon personal privacy and humiliation. This connection is especially close when the encroachment is institutional. There are, of course, personal encroachments upon the privacy of other individuals, from peeping to malicious gossip, but these encroachments are more relevant to the question of whether the society is civilized than whether it is decent. Later I will compare gossip societies to totalitarian societies with respect to the nature of their violation of personal privacy. The demand for the protection of privacy may come not only from individuals but also from institutions and firms that want to protect information concerning their vital interests from being made public. Here we are concerned with the privacy of individuals, not of institutions.

There is a direct conceptual link between the notion of decency and securing the separation of the public and the private spheres. Exposing to the public eye behavior or objects belonging to the private sphere is an indecent act. I remember one sunny day on Hampstead Heath, when

Londoners were exposing themselves to the sun. Two women were lying there, one in her underwear—white bra and panties—and the other in a bikini. An elderly Englishwoman near me got angry and exclaimed how indecent it was to strip like the woman in her underwear.

"And what about the one in the bikini?" I asked her.

"That's different," she responded. "Underwear is private."

As attested by this story, the question of what is perceived as the private and what as the public sphere is culture-dependent. The elderly Englishwoman had already learned to live with what had been scandalous in her youth—stripping in the park. But she had not learned to live with underwear exposed to everyone's eyes, as this has a strong association with private parts. The boundaries of the private and the public are dependent on culture and history. There are differences in the area of privacy not only between cultures and social classes, but also within the same culture at different historical times. Although the limits of the private undergo continual changes, the very division between a sphere hidden from the public eye and a sphere open to everyone is not dependent on society or culture. This is a distinction that cuts across all cultures. There is no one area of privacy that is in the private sphere in all cultures, but each culture has its own private sphere. This sphere may be very limited—having sexual relations in private, or performing one's bodily functions in private, or concealing one's private parts, and the like—but it is always there.

The claim that every culture makes a distinction between what is public and what is private is an empirical hypothesis, not a conceptual claim. The basis for my belief in this hypothesis comes from anthropological studies of societies in which there is great difficulty maintaining a private sphere owing to the conditions of life—for example, an Eskimo igloo. During the winter storms everyone lives within the closed igloo, so that even their bodily functions must be performed within this enclosed space, yet there is impressive evidence that they are nonetheless able to maintain an area of privacy in this setting. The Eskimos are extremely reluctant to expose their private parts. They perform sexual intercourse in total silence. They take care of their bodily functions in such a way that they cannot be seen. And they zealously guard their thoughts and their feelings about others and refuse to answer personal questions.[1]

There is an intimate connection between privacy and sexuality in the sense that in our culture sex is considered the most essentially private area. This explains, for example, why the Woodstock rock festival, as a manifestation of the counterculture, challenged our culture's basic premise that sexual relations must be kept away from the public eye. The connection between sex and privacy is not conceptual but historical. Its importance lies in the fact that we learn about privacy from sexual behavior, and not the other way around. The connection between sexuality and privacy, between privacy and modesty, is so strong that we tend to discuss privacy through examples taken from the sexual domain. But in our account privacy includes areas of activity that are not only, or even primarily, limited to the sexual domain. This domain nonetheless provides prototypical examples for a discussion of privacy.

The key question for our discussion is what is humiliating about the violation of privacy. The question is not what is bad about the violation of privacy in general, but what, if anything, is humiliating about it. Let us remember that we suggested two central motifs with respect to humiliation. The first is rejection, that is, exclusion from the "Family of Man." The second is denial of control. The concept of humiliation as loss of control is the operative concept of degradation as the destruction of human autonomy. Violation of privacy must be considered humiliation in both senses, but the second motif is more immediate, so I will begin with it.

The private realm is defined as the minimal sphere for individuals' control over their interests. Violation of privacy is restricting individuals' control, against their will, over what is supposed to be within their control. A society that permits institutional surveillance of the private sphere—by means of wiretapping, for example, or censoring letters, or other sorts of detective work—is doing many shameful things. One of these, though not the only one, is humiliation.

The question we must ask here is whether every systematic violation of privacy constitutes humiliation. There are two sorts of society which invade the individual's privacy in two different ways: the totalitarian society and the gossip society. A gossip society makes use of gossip for "social supervision." Such a society's intervention in the individual's privacy, even if it is humiliating, does not constitute institutional humiliation, unless we consider gossip columns institutions. It therefore involves the civilized rather than the decent society. The comparison between the civilized and the decent society is meant to highlight those aspects of the violation of privacy by totalitarian institutions that make it particularly humiliating, thus making totalitarian societies blatantly nondecent ones.

The violation of privacy in totalitarian regimes is not intended merely to uncover possible conspiracies against the regime. It also has the purpose of gathering information whose public revelation would embarrass or shame or humiliate the victim, so that the information can be used as blackmail. The humiliating outcome can thus take one of two forms. On the one hand, if the information about the person is revealed, it will present her in a bad light that is liable to lead to her rejection from society. On the other hand, the person may be forced into a nasty compromise—a compromise of her integrity—in which she gives in to the regime in order to prevent it from revealing this information. In such a case the victim is forced to compromise on her principles, say by disclosing secrets of her associates. In this description of the violation of privacy, it is not the act of violation that is intended to humiliate the victim. Rather, the violation of privacy is an efficient and powerful tool intended to serve other means of humiliation.

Another claim, inspired by Michel Foucault, says that violation of privacy has a normalizing surveillance function, channeling members of the society into standard behavior and turning deviates into perverts. Violation of privacy for the purpose of discovering deviance has as its goal the rejection of deviates and exceptions. The humiliation lies in turning the deviate into someone who does not satisfy the criteria of a normal human being, where only the normal can be considered human. The deviate is therefore rejected from humanity. A related claim is that the function of normalizing human behavior through surveillance, by means of the invisible eye, is one of the signs of modern society. The society's total institutions, such as prisons and mental hospitals, are prototypical examples of the trend of normalizing supervision which excludes deviates from human society.

Gossip breeds belonging and familiarity, which in turn breed contempt. Gossip in an intimate traditional society, even if it is explicit and revealing, takes for granted the human weaknesses of its victims. Traditional gossip is democratic. It creates a democracy of sufferers: "Don't think so highly of yourself. We know· your weaknesses, large and small." Violation of privacy in traditional gossip societies is not meant to exclude people from the society, let alone from humanity in general. On the contrary, gossip based partly on violation of privacy creates a sticky sense of belonging. In contemporary totalitarian societies the standard for being human is some model of the "new man" as conceived by the totalitarian ideology underlying the regime. In traditional gossip societies there is intimacy and acceptance of human weaknesses.

In gossip societies of the masses the violation of privacy affects mainly the rich and the famous. Famous people in such societies are often protected by high walls and body-guards. Only the high-powered lens of the paparazzi permits us to see the unflattering potbellies and bald spots of celebrities. The typical victims of such societies are powerful, famous people. But even such people have human dignity, and in a decent society they can and should be allowed to protect their dignity. The question, however, is whether gossip puts famous people in their place as basically ordinary people—insulting them, perhaps, but not humiliating them—or whether it actually makes them seem nonhuman. Does gossip affect only the celebrities' public image, or does it affect their self-image as well? One immediate answer, which does not get us very far, is that it depends on the type of gossip. Heinrich Böll, in his book *Die verlorene Ehre der Katharina Blum,* tried to show how a simple person is turned into a nonperson by the media's invasion of her privacy. Katharina Blum is a concentrate of reality rather than a typical case, but it is clear that if one is not protected by the armor of power and fame, the invasion of one's privacy will undermine one's self-respect.

The association between humiliation and the violation of privacy may be found in three separate but related issues: (1) violation of privacy can serve as an extreme form of humiliation in that those whose privacy is violated are shown that they lack even minimal control over their lives; (2) violation of privacy can be an expression of the fact that it makes no difference if the victims do or do not have control over their lives; and (3) violation of privacy can cause people to lose control over their lives. I have concentrated mainly on the causal relation between the violation of privacy and humiliation in the sense of loss of control, but humiliation does not necessarily require such a causal connection—it is enough that it is an expression of loss of control.

The area of privacy is culture-dependent in that different cultures may set its boundaries in different places. Whatever the bounded area, however, it is clear that the very declaration that this is the private arena means that it is the minimal area under the individual's control. Invasion of the private arena may be an effective restriction of control; or it may be intended to show the individual that he has no control, not even over this limited area; or it may be meant to show that it makes no difference whether he has any control or not. There is thus a tight link between the violation of privacy and one of the important senses of humiliation—namely, the sense involving the absence of minimal control.

A decent society in the sense of a nonhumiliating society is characterized on its basic institutional level by the fact that it does not violate the privacy of the individuals in the society.

Intimacy

Violation of privacy sometimes constitutes a death blow to the possibility of intimacy, where intimacy is a constitutive element of friendship. Destroying the possibility of friendship means destroying the possibility of the most significant belonging relationship in human life, except perhaps for the relationship of belonging to a family. Humiliation is the rejection of a person from a group based on significant belonging. Here instead of rejection there is destruction, or at least severe impairment, of the possibility of forming the most significant belonging relationship.

Two different concepts of friendship must be distinguished (I owe this distinction to Allen Silver). One is friendship based on the ability to rely on one another in times of trouble. This sort of friendship of reliance is characteristic of a group of warriors, and is maintained among the veterans of combat units ("I can wake him up in the middle of the night and he'll come without asking why"). The other is friendship based on shared intimacy, in which an important element is revealing one's deep secrets, whose exposure to the public eye would make one extremely vulnerable. The value of this intimate information—the "secrets"—lies in its scarcity, in its being a commodity saved for one's friends. Exposing secrets to anonymous observers is an immediate devaluation of their scarcity. People do, of course, reveal intimate information to strangers for the purpose of medical treatment or legal assistance, but it is a forced exposure for a specific purpose. Sharing one's secrets with a friend, in contrast, is a significant act constitutive of friendship. It is not merely a search for sympathy, or a cheap way to get therapy. Violation of privacy thus harms friendship based on intimacy more than friendship based on reliance in times of trouble.

As mentioned, totalitarian societies are interested in intimate information in order to exploit the vulnerability of their subjects. They are not particularly interested in apolitical intimacy, unless it reveals weaknesses that can be exploited for blackmail. Gossip societies are interested in intimate information for its own sake—it is the content that supports gossip. Totalitarian societies are interested in foiling friendships that might turn into alliances against the regime. The regime tries to penetrate the delicate fabric of the relations between people who stand by one another, on the model of "Divide and rule." The regime thus becomes the supreme arbiter of relationships between people. This is its totalitarian significance. In totalitarian regimes at times of great terror—as expressed, for example, in Nadezhda Mandelstam's descriptions of the Stalinist terror—the first victim of the terror is friendship. The feeling of degradation exists not only in those who made nasty compromises and betrayed their friends in times of trouble, but also in the people who were betrayed. Even if the latter preserved their integrity, they were witness to the destruction of their sense of belonging.

Yet there seems to be an observation that counters what I have described so far. Totalitarian societies have proved to be a prescription for and guarantor of brave friendship, since friendships in regimes of this sort are conspiracies of humanity against the inhumanity of the regime. Anyone who has ever known Soviet dissidents is moved by the intensity of their friendships. It is rather the downfall of these regimes that has hurt these veteran friendships. Everyone is left on his own. But dissidents are not a representative sample of anything. We must remember that by the time the dissidents appeared the totalitarian nature of these regimes had become unrecognizably weakened in comparison with the terrifying reality of the Stalinist era. Besides, we would have to clarify the nature of the friendships in regimes of terror: Are they friendships of reliance or of shared intimacy? I would not be surprised to find out that they are mainly of the first type—friends in need.

So far I have attempted to find out what aspect of the violation of privacy constitutes an act of humiliation, thus making it a marker of a nondecent society. The suggestions of blackmail, nasty compromise, the rejection of deviates, the destruction of intimacy and thus of a significant feeling of belonging, are all indirect answers to a question that seems to demand a direct response. And the answer that suggests itself is that the violation of privacy in itself is a paradigmatic act of humiliation. Searching people's private parts against their will is the prototypical example of a humiliating gesture. In the absence of a serious security justification, such as exists in the case of body searches at airports, which may be unwanted by the subjects but are done with their agreement and understanding, searching a person's private parts without his agreement is an extreme form of humiliation. The violation of privacy is an extension of this act.

In other words, self-respect and humiliation are based on a private space whose invasion is a symbolic act interpreted as humiliation, in the sense of the lack of consideration for the victim's vital interests. Inability to protect one's private zones is a sign of absolute helplessness in defending one's basic interests. It is also decisive evidence of a total lack of consideration on the part of the privacy invaders. Radical lack of consideration for our interests is an expression of lack of consideration for us as people. Which particular acts are considered an invasion of privacy—whether privacy is defined spatially or some other way—is culture-dependent, but the invasion of privacy is always a central act of humiliation. This is true even before this act is given an interpretation, such as lack of consideration for one's interests. In short, the fact that the physical aspect of invasion of privacy is a prototypical act of humiliation is one of the things that need little proof. There are many bad things involved in the violation of privacy, but our problem is limited to one specific thing—humiliation.

13

Bureaucracy

There are three issues of concern to people studying bureaucracy. The first is what bureaucracy is. This question is one of definition or explication: Is the staff of a large private insurance company, for example, considered a bureaucracy? The second issue is what constitutes a good bureaucracy. This normative question can take two different forms: one, how to characterize the tasks according to which a bureaucracy is judged; the other—a comparative question—how a public bureaucracy performs its tasks in comparison to the way similar tasks are performed in firms operating in a competitive market. Finally, the third issue is what makes bureaucracy work: What leads to the spread of bureaucracy? Do bureaucracies operate according to laws like the "Peter Principle" or "Parkinson's Law" (one version of which states that subordinates multiply at a fixed rate regardless of the amount of work produced)? Is "Yes, Minister" a caricature or a slice of reality?

The question of concern to us, however, is a different one: Which sort of bureaucracy, if any, is compatible with the decent society? The general answer should be obvious by now: the sort of bureaucracy that does not systematically humiliate those dependent on it. The purpose of the restricting term "systematically" is to distinguish between humiliation stemming from the nature of the bureaucracy and humiliation based on the random behavior of a few rotten officials who taint the whole institution of officialdom.

Answering our question involves the entire triple-level analysis of bureaucracy—the definitional, normative, and factual levels. For example, the definitional problem arises when we take into account the fact that the greatest student of bureaucracy, Max Weber, defines a bureaucrat as a person who has authority within his office.[1] Weber distinguishes between clerks and administrators: only the latter have authority in the office as decision makers. He thus considers only them to be bureaucrats, that is, representatives of the official authorities. This distinction greatly restricts the everyday concept of bureaucracy, as the people in need of clerical services come into contact precisely with the clerks whom Weber does not consider part of the bureaucracy. My use of the term does not follow Weber's. It includes not only officials who are called decision makers but the entire range of clerical workers. Here the term 'bureaucracy' includes not only public office workers financed by public money but also the clerical staff of firms that enjoy a monopoly or near-monopoly in the economy. In other words, bureaucracy includes all officials imposed on the public—imposed in the sense that individuals in the society have no alternative to them, whereas they do have alternatives to the officials in competitive or quasi-competitive businesses.

To avoid undesirable influences on our discussion, we

have to factor out the varying trends in people's attitudes toward bureaucracy. Bureaucracy has a bad name. At best it is considered a necessary evil, and always a partially superfluous evil. One of the main factors that give the welfare state a bad name is its essential dependence on bureaucracy. The welfare state is based on transferring payments and providing services outside the free market, which by definition requires a bureaucracy—that is, a clerical system to arrange the payments and guarantee the services. Bureaucracy is the greatest problem of social democracies, and not only of totalitarian socialism. The problem is that realizing the ideal of distributive justice in social democracies requires the use of an irritating system.

There is a mutual relationship between bureaucracy and services in general, and this is especially so in the case of welfare services: it is a fact that cutting the bureaucracy leads to a cut in services. This should not be the case, since most bureaucratic systems are quite inefficient. It would therefore seem that it should be possible to cut the bureaucratic system without decreasing the level of service. But bureaucratic systems, as a matter of social fact, don't shrink that way. In order to prove how necessary they are, they shrink in the places that hurt the public most: hospitals, schools, and the like. Moreover, clerical systems that are not market systems are based on seniority and the perks that go with it. Workers are dismissed according to the principle of last in, first out, which is not the most efficient criterion.

These last remarks are all quite banal, but that doesn't make them wrong. The attitude of societies based on bureaucracies shifts from one extreme to the other: from the extreme of hostility toward the bureaucratic authority to the extreme of complaining whenever there is a cut in services. The second extreme does not necessarily make the bureaucracy well liked—it may only mitigate the hostility somewhat.

The question troubling us is not whether bureaucracy is irritating, but whether it contains humiliating elements. One complaint constantly reiterated against all bureaucracies involves its mechanistic quality. Bureaucracies are based on impersonal relations, and so they are indifferent to individuals and their suffering and remote from their individuality and uniqueness. This impersonal attitude often becomes an inhuman attitude. "To bureaucrats people are just numbers" or "Clerks only see the application forms and not the people behind them" are familiar expressions of this sort of criticism. That is, bureaucracies are accused of seeing human beings as nonhuman—as numbers, or forms, or "cases." This attitude of seeing persons in a machinelike manner is humiliating in its very essence (see Chapter 6).

What is interesting is that it is precisely the machinelike qualities of bureaucracy, such as its lack of a personal attitude, that were considered its greatest assets by Weber. The comparison he made was between feudalism, which was based entirely on favoritism, and the Wilhelminian bureaucracy, which was not based on discriminatory personal relations. Bureaucracy at its best avoids feudal whims. You can't play favorites with people you don't know.

There are two sorts of "sticking by the rules" in official settings, and both of them put the bureaucracy in a position where it can't win—at least, not gratitude. If your particular case is an exceptional one and your serious problem requires special attention, if you do not fit into one of the standard pigeonholes of rules governing your case, then you will be bitter about the lack of a personal interest that takes your particular circumstances into consideration. Rule-sticklers who insist on fitting you into the Procrustean bed of artificial standards make your blood boil. Of course, what you want is a consideration of your case that will work in your favor. If your particular case is carefully considered and then disqualified, insult will be added to injury. You do not want merely personal consideration but also the desired result. If, however, you exactly fit the criteria spelled out in the rules and you deserve some sort of benefit, there is nothing more enraging than some clerk's attempt to exercise discretion. Even the clerk's pretense of having some say in the matter arouses your anger, since one possible result of such pretense is that you will have to go along with it and demonstrate gratitude to the official for the "favor" of giving you what you actually deserve.

If having a personal attitude is not merely a matter of good manners and friendly behavior, but also involves discretion beyond following general rules, then perhaps it is wrong to criticize bureaucrats for lacking a personal attitude. A personal attitude does not guarantee a humane attitude, in the sense of a considerate one. Rules that do not leave any room for discretion by the clerk handling the case may well be fairer and based more on rights than on charity. But if the rules themselves are unfair or even vile, as in the case of the Nuremberg Laws, then breaking them for the benefit of the victims is all to the good. A society with vile rules and corrupt officials is preferable to a society with vile rules and strict officials. A personal touch obtained through bribery is preferable to a nondiscriminatory attitude in the application of discriminatory rules. But one must not generalize too far in the case of evil governments, since corrupt officials are liable to abuse all the more those unfortunates who do not have the means to bribe them. All good regimes are alike, while every bad regime is bad in its own way. With evil there is no room for generalizations.

Weber struggled with the comparison between feudalism and bureaucracy as two different ideal-types of government. In feudalism the judicial, economic, and organizational roles are held by the same people without specialization or professionalization. A feudal administration lives off concessions, not salaries. The ideal-type of bureaucracy, in contrast, excels in rules having general force (which led Hegel to claim that bureaucracy embodies the safeguarding of the general interest). In other words, there are rules which are valid for all members of the society. Bureaucracy is based on roles and rules rather than personal relations.

All this, as mentioned, is true of the ideal-types of bureaucracy and feudalism. Weber never considered the possibility of the monstrous combination of "feudal bureaucracy"—the government of the "nomenclatura," a government that doesn't care about anyone who isn't "one of us," but may be very personal and considerate of the special privileges of "our own people." This is an administrative system resembling medieval estates where the lower officials are dependent on the higher ones and feel a vassalic loyalty toward them. A feudal bureaucracy is a creation that operates on the two principles of personal relations and impersonal relations, which combine to form inhuman relations.

The essence of humiliation is treating human beings as nonhuman. Saying that people are being treated as animals, objects, or machines are accepted ways of saying that they are being treated as nonhuman. Bureaucracy gives us a new way of saying this—treating people as numbers or as application forms. These two new expressions, alongside the comparison of people to machines, constitute the modern ways of saying that people are being treated as nonhuman. That is, one way of expressing the modern type of humiliation is through the idea that people are seen as numbers. The most extreme manifestation of this idea was the tattoo inscribed by the Nazi bureaucracy on the arms of the prisoners in the concentration camps. A person's name is a label of her identity and she identifies with it in a deep sense. Causing a person to be ashamed of her name can be a serious act of humiliation. Systematically refusing to relate to a person by her name is a gesture of erasing her label of human identity. Referring metonymically to Magic Johnson as number 32, or to Larry Bird as number 33, may of course be an expression of supreme honor, since these shirt numbers have become their special symbols in the eyes of basketball fans. But replacing a person's name by a number in prison is an act of rejecting the person from society. It may mean rejecting the person from the Family of Man. This is the meaning of human beings as numbers.

One response may be to say that this is not a new way of treating people as nonhuman. Treating people as numbers may be seen as one manifestation of treating people as animals, since domestic animals are labeled by numbers branded on them. Alternatively, it can be seen as a manifestation of treating people as machines, since cars too are identified by their numbers.

In order to focus on the hard core of the notion that seeing human beings as numbers is another manifestation of treating them as nonhuman, we must distinguish between rejection and lack of recognition. This distinction will probably not be acceptable to everyone.[2]

The feeling of being treated as a number can be the expression of a person's sense that her treasured qualities are not appreciated and that she is being treated as if she were anonymous. That is, treating a person as a number can be an expression of lack of recognition that injures one's self-esteem rather than humiliation. But I am concerned with a more radical manifestation of treating a human being as a number, which expresses rejection of the person from the Family of Man and therefore affronts her dignity, thus constituting humiliation.

A person may feel insulted by the very request to fill out forms in which he has to fit himself into neutral categories that do not convey anything of what is precious about him, and he may experience it as being treated as a number. But I am interested in cases involving humiliation rather the insult of nonrecognition. Numbers are identification tags, and as such they are vital for running a modern society—including passport numbers, ID numbers, social security numbers, drivers' license numbers, and the like.

In premodern societies the very notion of counting people was sometimes considered a forbidden act, perhaps because it was perceived as an invitation to the evil eye or perhaps because it was seen as a manifestation of treating human beings as nonhuman. Cattle may be counted, but not human beings. Thus, for example, the Bible tells how King David was tempted to carry out a population census, thus committing a sin which brought a plague on the people (II Samuel 24). This may be true of traditional societies, but in modern societies it is hard to see how life can be conducted without the use of numerical categories and identifying tags.

Turning a human being into a number means changing an identification tag into a forced identity. This occurs when the only identity traits recognized by the society's institutions for an individual or a group are the numerical tags. If, for example, the only way the prison authorities refer to a prisoner is by the numerical label he wears, then he is really being treated as a number. Elias Canetti, a keen connoisseur of dehumanization in modern life, wrote a play *(The Numbered)* in which he describes a fictional society where the tag that has taken over people's lives is the number. The number, which is supposed to represent the date on which they are doomed to die, is recorded in a capsule hung around their neck. Mr. Fifty *(Fünfzig)* rebels and discovers that these capsules are actually empty. What he has found out is that the numerical labels are not connected with any real trait of these people, not even the date on which they are destined to die. Numerical identification tags are based on one's place in a sequence and not on any trait that a person can actually identify with. The numerical tag permits identification by others without a sense of identity on the part of the person wearing it. It is when the numerical tag is used at the

expense of identity that it is an expression of the treatment of human beings as numbers.

But whether treating people as numbers is an old or a
new manifestation of treating them as nonhuman, and
whether it is based on treating people as animals or as
machines, bureaucracy is liable to be perceived as treating
people in a humiliating way, akin to treating them as
numbers. It would be useful for my account of the decent
society to take a look at bureaucracy in action. One way
to do this is to examine its role in the welfare state.

14

The Welfare Society

Both the ideological sources and the actual background for the growth of the welfare state and the welfare society are issues that have been discussed in great detail by many.[1] The eclectic character of the idea of social welfare indicates that the sources of the welfare river must be sought in many streams: Christian, socialist, and statist (Bismarck). These have often led to conflicting notions of the character of the welfare society, and especially to conflicting justifications for the necessity of such a society. Some thinkers have justified the need for welfare services by arguing that they are needed for protecting the capitalist system—they provide a social safety net for losers in the economic race who might otherwise undermine the system. Other thinkers, in contrast, have seen the welfare state as a moderate form of socialism which is compatible with a market economy, but expropriates some important areas from the market, such as health, education, and pension funds.

My own interest in the welfare society centers on the question of the relationship between it and the decent society. Among the historical sources of the welfare idea is the notion of the necessity for eradicating degrading treatment of the poor, of the type embodied in England's Poor Laws. The English Poor Laws, in all their transformations from the time of Elizabeth I, played a part in the use of humiliation as a deterrent against the exploitation of welfare by people looking for a free meal. The idea was that providing people with the bread of charity would encourage laziness and undesired dependence on society. The way to deter lazy people from asking for support was by offering such support under particularly humiliating conditions. Anyone who could accept these debasing conditions would thus be someone without any choice. The phrase "rogue poor" was an expression of deep suspicion toward the penniless. This phrase was not just a remnant of the terrorism of wandering beggars in a society without street lighting. The suspicion was based on the belief that the poor are to blame for their situation. It was considered necessary to separate the swindling poor people who were actually capable of working, called paupers, from the deserving poor who could not help their situation. The way to make this distinction was through their willingness to live in poorhouses. There, in the poorhouses, strict discipline—which was nothing but a euphemism for moral abasement and humiliation—was employed for the purpose of improving the morals of the lazy, swindling poor. George Lansbury, after his first visit to the poorhouse of which he was about to become a trustee, wrote that "everything possible was done to inflict mental and moral degradation."[2] The poor were put to the test of the poorhouse while the one who really ought to have been put to that test, in the words of Dr. Johnson, was society as a whole: "A decent concern for the poor is the true test of civilization."[3]

My detour into the world of Dickens is not an archaism irrelevant to the present-day world. Suspicion of the sham poor, who are nothing but lazy exploiters dipping their vampiric fingers into the public's pockets, still nourishes opposition to the welfare state and those in need of it. The desire to put the needy to humiliating tests of entitlement is not entirely a thing of the past. The Dickensian reality may have vanished from developed welfare states, but the desire to use humiliating tests as a deterrent to false demands and requests still exists.

I have presented one of the historical motives for the establishment of the welfare state as the desire to eliminate the humiliating manner in which support was given to the poor in societies relying on philanthropy. But one complaint against the welfare society is that it too is humiliating. Not only does it not prevent humiliation, it actually causes humiliation through its own institutions. The welfare society creates dependent people lacking in self-respect, who are willing to sell their birthright of personal autonomy and pride for a bowl of lentils from the public kitchen. It is a paternalistic society that takes upon itself the right to replace people's judgment about what is good for them by its own discretion. It is a society that perpetuates the second-class citizenship of the needy and gives them the practical status of nonadult human beings. The conclusion is thus that a decent society must not be a welfare society, because welfare societies are demeaning.

We are faced with two conflicting claims: on one view, the welfare society is a necessary condition for a decent society, because only the welfare society has the power to eradicate the institutional humiliation that disqualifies a society from being a decent one. On the opposing view, the welfare society is itself debasing, and its humiliation is institutional, so that it cannot be a decent society.

Let us first discuss the claim that the welfare society is an essential complement of the decent society because it provides a safeguard against degrading life conditions such as poverty, unemployment, and illness. A considerable part of the discussion focuses on the question of whether poverty, unemployment, and illness are actually humiliating life conditions. We must keep in mind that our present interest in the welfare society is limited to the question of whether it prevents or promotes humiliation.

Poverty and Humiliation

We must first distinguish between the welfare state and the welfare society. A welfare state is a society in which the state is the provider of welfare services. A welfare society is one in which voluntary, or quasi-voluntary, organizations provide these services. The State of Israel, for example, is a welfare state. The Jewish Settlement in Palestine at the time of the British Mandate constituted a welfare society. We are discussing the welfare society, but the most convenient way to illustrate it is through the example of the welfare state.

Humiliation is not necessarily the outcome of an intent to humiliate. It can be the outcome of life conditions brought about by institutions or individuals. For example, a recession that leads to unemployment may well be the planned result of an anti-inflationary monetary policy, but it may just as well be—and in most cases is—an unintended outcome of economic behavior. A welfare society is supposed to ameliorate not only intentional humiliation but also degrading life conditions, such as unemployment, that are not generally the result of planning.

Not every sort of human distress is a cause of humiliation. The question is how we can judge when the life conditions of human distress are to be considered humiliating. Poverty is a prototypical case for testing the problem of when to call certain states of affairs or life conditions humiliating—states of affairs that are the result of human action, but without the intention to humiliate anyone. Our focused question, then, is whether poverty as such is humiliating.

The question is not whether poor people feel humiliated, but whether they have a sound reason for feeling that way. Harsh poverty may dull the feeling of degradation, but that would not eliminate the justification for it. The way I have chosen to discuss this question is through a poem of Hayyim Nahman Bialik's. A poem is not an argument, but it can be turned into one. Bialik's poem "Widowhood," in which the poet is pained by his widowed mother's poverty, contains an implicit argument in addition to a devastating description of destitution.

The poet has no doubt that poverty is humiliating, "for Man's grandeur is defiled." He even challenges God: "How did God see and forbear as the glory of his image on earth turned demon of destruction?" Human dignity is described as being created in God's image, and this dignity has been destroyed. These poetic utterances are an emphatic version of the view that poverty is humiliating. But Bialik also provides a description of the aspects of poverty in virtue of which it is humiliating:

> Upon the ruins of her house and her life's desolation she suddenly was displayed,
> Exposed and empty of all, without shelter or security
> . . . . .
> Alone and without means of defense, abandoned to her soul and her failure
> . . . . .
> A worm among human worms like her, creatures grieved and oppressed.
> . . . . .
> Women embittered and wretched,
> Twisted of form and dreadful of mien,
> . . . . .
> Divested of grace and mercy, obliterated of any semblance of mother and wife,
> A crippled rabble . . . Enraged by cats of prey howling for ferocious skirmish
> Over every bone broken open and every piece of putrid meat flung casually before them.

> (translated by Harold Schimmel)

The aspects of degrading poverty that corrode human dignity are exposure, lack of shelter; being "alone and without means of defense," that is, total vulnerability and helplessness; abandonment to failure; the battle for life, which is a dog-eat-dog battle over a thrown bone, being lowered to a bestial level in a desperate battle for existence; loss of the semblance of womanhood and motherhood, inability to provide food for one's children. All these are joined by filth; loss of normal physical appearance, loss of interest and desire for life; insulting crudeness— "covered by the dung of the mouths" of those with whom she is competing for existence, the lack of basic human sisterhood among the suffering women; humiliation on the part of those who "casually" throw the "bone broken open," the "putrid meat," without compassion or sympathy, but as if they were throwing a bone to a homeless dog.

Standing in contrast to this view of poverty as humiliating is early Christianity's view of poverty, even at its most wretched, as ennobling: "[To the poor] is the kingdom of heaven" (Matthew 5:3). The idea is that what prevents humans from fulfilling their noble vocation as the possessors of a soul is material possessions. To be poor means to be liberated from all the trappings and traps of materialism, and so it is elevating rather than corrupting. Society's problem is not how to eliminate humiliation by eliminating poverty, but how to remove the humiliation from poverty.

As to the possibility of eliminating poverty itself, both Christians and Jews face a contradictory text. In Deuteronomy we find two views expressed in the very same chapter (chapter 15). On the one hand, the view that guided devout Puritans and Victorians is expressed in verse 11: "For there will never cease to be needy ones in your land." On the other hand, the view that a society without poverty is possible is expressed in verse 4: "There shall be no needy among you."

Noble poverty requires two conditions: one, that the poor are not responsible for a family; and two, that the poverty is voluntary. In both Christianity and Buddhism noble poverty is the poverty of the monk and the nun. A reevaluation of poverty, in the sense of removing the humiliation from it, is bound to be limited to voluntary poverty and the poverty of the childless.

Reevaluation of poverty as noble is like the Stoic attitude in its Cynic form. What I wrote at the beginning of this book about the Stoic attitude toward humiliation, or, more precisely, about the Stoic belief that slavery is not humiliating, is also true about the notion of noble poverty.

The notion of poverty is relative. A person who is poor in California may be well-to-do in Calcutta. But being poor does not mean being in the lowest decile of income. Poverty is not defined relative to income distribution, but to the social concept of the minimal conditions of existence. This minimum is connected to the social conception of what is needed for living a human life. The minimum reflects the concept of humanity prevalent in each society. It also reflects the idea of a threshold for economic citizenship in the society.

So far I have kept apart the notions of self-esteem and self-worth. But when it comes to setting a threshold for self-esteem, it becomes very difficult to maintain such a separation—especially when poverty is defined as failure, a failure whose painful effect is that poverty might leave the poor without even one option for living a valuable life. Valuing a way of life does not require considering it a preferred way of life, but it does require at least one option for a way of life that the person can respect and finds worth living. Poverty closes off ways of life that people consider dignified. In addition, there is a sense that being poor is the fruit of total failure.

Throwing the blame of failure on the narrow shoulders

of the poor was one of the manifestations of self-righteousness in the Poor Laws. The changed attitude toward the
poor that led to the rise of the welfare society stems,
however, from a severe blow dealt to the idea of the poor
as responsible for their plight: business cycles in capitalist
economies have thrown too many people out of work for
it to remain credible that their poverty is the result of
laziness or drunkenness. Recruitment of the masses into
national armies also led to a change in attitude toward the
penniless recruits. These were suddenly perceived as having the power to contribute to the war effort. But although the claim that being poor is the result of a moral
defect has lost some of its strength, it still exists and serves
as a poisoned arrow in the attack on the welfare state.

The unjustified claim that poverty in general results
from failure on the part of the poor is first of all just
that—an unjustified claim. It also diminishes the social
honor of the poor. But why should the claim that a person's poverty means failure diminish the person's dignity
as a human being? Failing an examination that may be
crucial for one's career, whether or not this failure can be
excused, prevents the person, at least temporarily, from
achieving her preferred way of life. This failure may be
very painful, but it is no reason for rejecting the person
as a human being. Any reassessment of the person who
has failed, whether by the society or by the person herself,
is an evaluation of only one aspect of the human being,
albeit an important one. But seeing poverty as failure
implicitly includes a wholesale judgment of the person as
worthless, as someone who cannot secure even the minimum necessities for existence. Seeing poverty as closing
off possibilities of living that are worthwhile in the eyes of

the poor themselves makes them seem worthless to themselves as well, as if they are incapable of living a life that is worthwhile even in their own eyes. Total failure is liable to be perceived as failure as a human being, and not merely in a particular task. When the accusation of failure is baseless, it is especially cruel and wicked since it is also humiliating.

The conclusion is that poverty is humiliating. The welfare state was created to eradicate poverty or at least to eliminate some of its humiliating features. The welfare society attempts to do this differently than the charity society, which relies on pity as the emotion motivating people to give to the poor.

Pity

Poverty is an important issue in a charity society, where poor people are given charity, whether directly or through public but voluntary charity collections. The emotion that motivates the charity society—as distinct from the emotion that is supposed to justify it—is pity. The founders of the welfare society intended it to eliminate the feeling of pity as a motive and a justification for supporting the needy.

The poor are given charity out of pity—not solely out of pity, but pity plays an important part in giving alms. Begging for alms is humiliating. The rabbis, in their commentary on the Torah, attempted to mitigate the humiliating aspect of begging from door to door by saying, "God stands with the poor person at the door" (Midrash Leviticus Rabbah). But the attempt to mitigate the humiliation does not succeed even when the almsgiver acts with a willing heart. The basic situation of begging for alms is humiliating. In contrast, mercy is considered an ennobling emotion, and the quality of mercy one of the higher human qualities. The attribute of mercy is the first of the thirteen attributes of God (see Exodus 34:6–7), and in Jewish prayer God is called "the merciful Father." The tension is palpable: on the one hand, mercy is an uplifting quality for the giver; on the other hand, being on the receiving end of mercy is humiliating. This tension is inherent in mercy, which vacillates between pity and compassion.

A strong advocate of reevaluating the emotion of pity *(Mitleiden)* was Nietzsche.[4] His critique of pity as a moral emotion has particular weight as a criticism of the charity society. The welfare society attempts to respond to the problems which the charity society was designed to solve, but without relying on pity. When Nietzsche called for a reevaluation of all values he was not merely demanding that accepted values be replaced by new ones. He was demanding a second-order evaluation of first-order values—that values seen as desirable should now be seen as undesirable, and vice versa. The criterion for evaluating values is to see what strengthens and what weakens human self-perfection. This is the way to understand Nietzsche's criticism of pity morality. Morality must begin, according to Nietzsche, with a reflexive attitude in which the individual takes steps to perfect himself. Only if the individual truly cares about his own authenticity can he be generous toward others. The sort of morality that begins with pity causes the individual to run away from himself to a sentimental posture toward the other. Sentimentality is an emotion which, according to Nietzsche, lacks the cruelty needed for a sober view of what can really be done to help the other. The opposite of altruism is not egoism but self-perfection. Perfecting oneself requires the individual to change his values with respect to his accepted notions of pride. In lieu of these accepted notions he must acquire a notion of pride befitting the overman (*Übermensch*).

Nietzsche was not the first to criticize the emotion of pity. Spinoza did so long before him,[5] claiming that it is based on a metaphysical illusion: just as one does not pity an infant for not being able to speak, so one should not pity a person's defects. Such defects are the result of the same sort of necessity that prevents the infant from talking. But for our purposes Nietzsche is the relevant critic of the emotion of pity, since he compares it with human dignity. The problem is that Nietzsche compares pity with the wrong sort of human dignity—the honor and pride of the overman. The concept of honor that concerns us is the honor of human beings as they actually are. The important questions for the present discussion are: What's wrong with pitying those in need? What's wrong with this emotion if it effectively motivates people to help those in distress? Why is pity so bad that a decent society must not be based on helping others out of pity? And, finally, is there a sound reason to consider yourself humiliated when other people pity you? You undoubtedly suffer from the problem for which you are pitied, but why should you also consider yourself humiliated?

The relation of pity is not a symmetric one. There is a feeling of superiority built into the emotion of pity: "It happened to you, but it can't happen to me." It is this asymmetry that distinguishes pity from compassion. Compassion is potentially a symmetric relation. When someone performs an act of charity out of pity, there is an implicit assumption that the one benefiting from it ought to be grateful. The feeling of pity does not leave room for the possibility that the pitier herself might need pity some day. On the contrary, the pitier implicitly assumes that she is inherently superior to the person she is pitying. Her pity is formed from a protected standpoint, as if she were immune to trouble and distress. When the pitier's standpoint is not protected in this way, the relation is transformed from pity to compassion. The distinction I am making between "pity" and "compassion" is not generally maintained: the two words are often used interchangeably. But it is a distinction with merit.

Recipients of pity have a sound basis for suspecting that they are not being respected, because what triggers pity are helplessness and vulnerability. If people are in control, they are not pitied even when they are in severe distress. Pity is accorded to people who have lost important sources of self-esteem, bordering on the loss of the means of defending their self-respect.

Nietzsche, that sharp-eyed critic of pity, claims that this emotion is directed toward Man's animal nature, toward what humans and animals have in common. Pity is not based predominantly on Man's human aspect. One pities a person the way one pities a suffering animal—a yelping dog, a cat yowling with hunger, a caged sparrow. In short, pity is predominantly a response to physical suffering. The poor who are the objects of the sentimental attitude of pity become incarnations of innocence, like sad-eyed lassoed horses. Sentimentality fakes emotions by presenting its objects as incarnations of innocence, lacking their own will or personality. One of the bad things about pity is what's bad about sentimentality in general: both of them morally distort the nature of their objects.

The words "piety" and "pity" are both derived from the Latin *pietas*, but they have become semantically differentiated in English. Piety is a religious sentiment which includes unconditional obligation toward the other (especially sufferers) that comes from a sincere religious consciousness. The religious claim is that the truly just society is based on piety rather than pity—on an obligation to the poor derived from Man's obligation to God, rather than condescension toward the poor. Nietzsche's inability to have this feeling might seem to religious people as a fault of Nietzsche's rather than a problem with the feeling.

Of course, Nietzsche would not have accepted the distinction between piety and pity. But whatever Nietzsche's position might be, my own obligation is to base the decent society on the humanist assumption. A just society based on piety does not satisfy this condition.

In summary, the welfare state tries to eliminate the humiliation born of pity on two levels: it attempts to eliminate the degrading life conditions of poverty, or at least to mitigate them substantially. Moreover, it tries to eliminate poverty itself without making use of the insulting and perhaps also humiliating motive of pity, the emotion which motivates the charity society.

The Welfare Society as a Humiliating Society

Ludwig von Mises was no friend of the welfare state, but he was aware of the humiliating elements in the charity society it purports to replace:

> The indigent has no legal claim to the kindness shown
> to him. He depends on the mercy of benevolent people,
> on the feelings of tenderness which his distress arouses.
> What he receives is a voluntary gift for which he must
> be grateful. To be an almsman is shameful and humili-
> ating. It is an unbearable condition for a self-respecting
> man.[6]

Von Mises was skeptical, however, that replacing almsgiv-
ers by the officials of the welfare state could make the
crooked straight. He declared a tie between the humiliation of the indigent in the welfare society and in the
charity society. We are interested in finding out whether
the competition between the philanthropist and the bureaucrat, between the charity society and the welfare society, really ends in a tie, or whether the welfare society
either ameliorates or worsens the humiliation of the needy
inherent in the charity society.

Comparing the philanthropist and the official as representatives of the charity society and the welfare society,
respectively, presupposes that the welfare society is essentially bureaucratic. Thus the complaints directed against
the welfare society are mostly the same ones that are
directed against bureaucracy's humiliating potential. If
the welfare society is really bureaucratic by its very nature,
then I have no need to recycle what I have already said
about the humiliating elements in bureaucracy. Everything said there applies to the welfare society as well.

We have already discussed the argument that there is a
necessary connection between welfare and bureaucracy.
The welfare society attempts to improve the situation of
the handicapped, the old, the unemployed, and the poor
without making use of the market mechanism. It thus

requires a clerical staff that is not supported and regulated by the market. This staff is responsible for providing services and transferring payments to the needy. Bureaucracy is thus built into the structure of the welfare society. The terms "bureaucracy" and "clerical staff" conjure up a picture of an entire system consisting of coffee-drinking clerks sitting behind desks. But the people taking care of the needy in a welfare society are of many different types: nurses, social workers, and the like. Of course, this is only true in cases where the welfare society provides the services itself and does not consist entirely of a clerical staff that transfers payments to the poor to buy their own services on the market. A welfare society that is restricted in the extent of its services does not necessarily restrict the amounts of money it gives the needy. In such a society the application of the notion of bureaucracy is restricted to the narrow sense, as including only officials. A welfare society based solely on transfer payments has a much more restricted bureaucracy, but it too cannot exist without any bureaucracy at all.

Aside from the claim that the problem with the welfare society is its bureaucratic nature, which diminishes the self-respect of those requiring its services, there are other complaints about the welfare society. One central complaint about a humiliating aspect of the welfare society is that it impairs the autonomy of the needy. It turns them into parasites drugged by public funds who are no longer able to rely on themselves. The money provided by welfare services is easy money from the point of view of the needy. They do not work for it, and so they are strongly motivated to remain dependent on the welfare services rather than stand on their own feet. As they have already made the humiliating move of accepting these services, they feel that they might as well enjoy the "dividends" of their humiliation.

The welfare state thus deprives the needy of the ability and authority to decide their own affairs, and hands over decisions that should express the individual's autonomy to paternalistic officials. This criticism of the welfare state nonetheless recognizes that if it hands over transfer payments instead of providing the services itself, it is less humiliating than the ordinary welfare state; it allows the needy to make decisions relevant to their lives.

One counterargument to this claim is that the poor do not simply require income supplements; what they need are specific services and products. Poverty is often associated with a culture of poverty. One of its manifestations is that the poor have an order of priorities which does not reflect what they really need. The stereotypical complaint is that poor men are liable to spend their income supplements on alcohol instead of medicine for their children. A negative income tax increases the consumption of the members of the poverty culture, but not of the necessities whose lack is what defines them as needy. What is consumed in a culture of poverty, such as drugs and alcohol, constitutes a breach of autonomy far more serious than any paternalistic intervention by well-meaning social workers.

When I referred above to the poor man's family I touched on a particularly important point. We often discuss human dignity as if society were composed of individuals making their own decisions for themselves, whereas in reality heads of families often make decisions that affect their dependents. Taking away part of the autonomy of the head of a household may perhaps serve to secure more autonomy for the other members of the family.

The conflicting arguments just presented gain their force from pictures of the welfare society which hold us captive. It is easy to go wrong here and identify the welfare society with our powerful stereotypes of its main protagonists: on the one hand, good-hearted social workers unconditionally devoted to the families they take care of; on the other hand, brutal night visits by supervisory authorities at the homes of single mothers to check whether there is a man hiding under the bed.

Most of the issues are factual ones to which I have nothing to contribute. The way I suggest of comparing the humiliating aspects of the charity society and the welfare society is by considering the ideal types of these two societies rather than their actual manifestations. By ideal types I mean not only types of people but also the principles guiding the charity as opposed to the welfare society. We must remember that the officials we associate with the welfare society do not belong exclusively to this type of society. Traditional charity societies were also often run by appointed officials, and not only by voluntary or elected charity collectors. Muslim charities in large cities, church charity collections, and the charity funds of traditional Jewish societies all possess a significant bureaucratic structure. Even the collection of the money is not based purely on voluntary contributions, but is a sort of taxation with considerable power to compel people to contribute. It makes very little difference if the compulsion to contribute is based on social pressure—in the form, say, of excommunication that might involve economic ruin—or institutional sanctions.

The emphasis is thus on comparing the principles guiding the two societies in the help they offer the needy. The charity society at its best is based on the principle of benevolence, the welfare society on the principle of entitlement. I claim that a society which assists the needy on the basis of their being entitled to the assistance is less humiliating in principle—whatever the application might be—than a society based on benevolence. As mentioned, this claim is based on ideal types that are more ideals than actual types. In the ideal sense the welfare society should be less humiliating than the charity society. But to claim that the charity society is motivated by the principle of benevolence does not mean that charity is actually given out of benevolence in the sense of being an act that is not obligatory. Charity is one of the important obligations of traditional charity societies. The idea is that even though the giver is obligated to give, the recipient receives the charity as a gift rather than as a right. In other words, obligations are disconnected from rights.

The Charity Paradox

The previous section may have given the impression that the charity and the welfare society differ solely in the motivations of the givers—that the question is whether they are motivated by benevolence (which conceals a sense of superiority) or by a sense of obligation toward needy people who are entitled to assistance. In the case of a welfare society based on rights, recipients of assistance are humiliated when officials act as though they are giving out of benevolence what the recipients are entitled to by right. The welfare society humiliates the needy when its officials treat them according to the norms of the charity society. We are interested in comparing the two societies at their best. The question is thus whether we can imagine a charity society based only on pure motives of providing assistance without humiliating the recipients, through a sincere concern for their well-being. If a charity society of this sort is possible, then giving alms in a humiliating way is nothing but a distortion of its true nature. This would be, as noted, a distortion of the charity society at its best, not a statistical deviation from the normal behavior of charity societies. What we must do is consider charity in the pure sense, and not as it appears in the guise of egotistical self-righteousness.

The question thus is whether a charity society based on pure benevolence is more capable than a welfare society of respecting the dignity of the needy. After all, the welfare society is based on allocating what was obtained by taxation, while the charity society at its best is based on voluntary donations. At first glance it would seem that this fact is enough to grant the charity society a great moral advantage over the welfare society.

When Richard Titmuss, the great student of the welfare society, was searching for a good model of how to give the needy what they require, he used the example of the social institution of the blood bank.[7] In other words, Titmuss's model was taken from the charity society at its best. The act of giving blood is immeasurably nobler than the act of selling it, yet the person who needs the blood does not consider herself humiliated in accepting blood donated out of benevolence. The conclusion is that giving blood is an example of the charity society at its best, and this sort of giving is preferable to any other sort of assistance to one's fellow human beings. If accepting donations of blood is not humiliating, then we must see to it that accepting donations of money should be considered equally respectable by the needy.

The counterargument states that one cannot infer from the example of giving blood that it is possible to donate money as well in a charity society without humiliation. Giving blood, says the counterargument, is very different from giving money or the equivalent of money. The recipient of the blood, in contrast to the recipient of the money, does not accumulate it, and the donor does not miss it. There is no element of greed in the case of blood. Having more blood in one's body is not a source of social prestige. Thus willingness to give blood has a different meaning than willingness to give money to the poor. It is impossible for the recipient to waste the blood or spend it on something it was not intended for. The blood donor, in contrast to the donor of the money, did not do anything to become the owner of the blood. It is true that she could have considered selling the blood, but in considering this possibility she does not see herself as having invested anything in it. Blood donors see themselves as saving lives. There is an immediate dramatic impact to giving blood, whereas there is rarely such an impact in giving money to the poor. But the main point is that blood donors can easily see themselves as needing blood one day, whereas donors of money do not easily see themselves as needing donations of money from others.

Moreover, aside from the differences in the act of giving itself, giving blood is not a good model of charity societies from the standpoint of the way the system is run. In some countries blood donations are considered a form of insurance, where the family or friends of a patient in need of blood donate units to make up the shortfall. There is no analogous possibility in the case of donating money, since poor people's friends are generally as poor as they are. The conclusion is that giving blood cannot tell us anything about the way we ought to provide people with financial assistance.

But one can rebut this counterargument as well. One can claim that it is precisely the giving of blood that is instructive as a possible social paradigm for donating money in a decent society. The reason is that in order to give or receive blood people have to overcome deeply entrenched prejudices: magical beliefs, rituals, and racism, all of which are connected with blood. The prejudices associated with blood are also associated with honor and humiliation. It was the Castilian nobility who arrogantly claimed to have "blue blood" *(sangre azul)*—blood unadulterated by the "dark blood" of Jews and Muslims. As evidence, these nobles displayed their blue veins, which could be seen through their pale skin.

But Castilian blue blood is ancient history now. Let us take a look at more recent history. During World War II the Red Cross still separated the blood of whites and blacks. I mention these facts in order to stress the prejudices that blood banks had to overcome. The idea of being related "by blood" is a deep, dark concept that refers to tribal, family, and even national kinship. Yet, wonder of wonders, donating blood is now universal. The only important factor is the biological one of blood types. When these facts, which show how ancient prejudices can be overcome, are taken into account, they should strengthen our faith that giving blood is a possible model of nonhumiliating social generosity that could be emulated in other charity-related areas as well.

So far we have discussed two points. The first is the issue of the motive for almsgiving, and particularly the possibility of a purely altruistic motive—generosity without self-righteousness. The second issue, which is connected with the first, is the question of whether giving blood can serve as a model of pure charity in a fine spirit of voluntarism and generosity, without humiliation.

The charity paradox consists of the following conundrum: Is it preferable (with a view to avoiding insult and humiliation) for charity to be given out of good motives, or might it not be better for it to be given out of bad motives? Good motives are those concerned with the other person's well-being without the least tinge of selfishness. The donor gives to the needy purely out of concern for the other without asking for anything in return. Charity is its own reward. Bad motives for the present purposes are those where donors give to the needy out of the selfish consideration of how they, the donors, will be seen and regarded by other people. This is a bad motive because it makes use of someone else's suffering to raise one's own status in one's eyes and the eyes of others.

At first glance it seems simple: it's better to give out of good motives than out of bad ones. And indeed, that's how it looks from the donors' viewpoint, but our question is how it looks from the recipients' viewpoint. What is better for the recipients: to receive charity given out of good motives or out of bad motives?

From the recipients' viewpoint, if they are given charity from people with selfish motives, their very willingness to accept the gift provides the donors with selfish satisfaction, and so the recipients need not feel that they owe the donors anything. They are obligated to express their thanks but not to feel gratitude. One is obliged to feel gratitude only toward donors who give out of exclusive concern for the recipients. The donors cannot actually ask for gratitude, since they did not act for the sake of receiving it, but the recipients on their part are obliged to feel gratitude because they have benefited from the donors' generosity. Feeling gratitude, yet being unable to return the kindness, tends to put people in an inferior position, as compared with their situation when they only owe their benefactors lip service because the latter acted out of selfish considerations.

One might think that people who are prepared to give charity out of pure altruism would also be willing to make their donations anonymously. This would liberate the recipients from the need to express gratitude, but it would not solve the problem. The problem is the *feeling* of gratitude, not the *words* of thanks. Recipients of anonymous gifts are exempt at most from expressing thanks, but not from feeling gratitude. The problem is admitting that they are in such an inferior situation that they are unable to return the kindness shown them. Moreover, the donors are in no need of any favors in return for their gifts. The principle of mutuality in gift-giving is broken. This principle lies at the heart of the charity problem, which cannot be solved even by anonymous donations. Selfish donors can be compensated, but altruistic donors cannot be. People would rather receive gifts from someone they can give to in return than from someone they cannot give anything to.

The charity paradox attests that even the charity society at its best—when based on the pure motive of helping others without a tinge of selfishness—is not free of insulting and possibly even humiliating aspects, precisely because of the purity of the donors' motives. Moreover, it is not certain that such a society can avoid humiliation better than a charity society based on the donors' selfish motives.

Two issues have been conflated here: the type of bureaucracy a society must have in order to be a decent one, and the connection between a welfare society dependent on bureaucracy and a decent society. The issues were clarified by a comparison of the way the welfare society and the charity society deal with the humiliating situation of poverty.

There are many dimensions along which the welfare society and the charity society could be compared: efficiency, extent of assistance, even their goals. I have focused, however, on only one issue—that of humiliation. If the welfare society wins this competition, it is a decision on points rather than a knockout. What I mean is that the charity society is not necessarily nondecent for humiliating by almsgiving, while a decent society is not necessarily a welfare society, but can also be a charity society.

15

Unemployment

Is a decent society one without unemployment? At first it would seem that unemployment should be discussed together with poverty, since unemployment is the absence of work that provides an income. It is bad to be unemployed not because you have no work but because you have no income. It would therefore seem that work is only a means of earning a livelihood and not an end that must be guaranteed by a decent society. Income must be guaranteed in order to prevent poverty, but employment is only one of the means of doing this.

But is this true? Is forced unemployment not humiliating in and of itself? Is it only the economic and social effects of unemployment that are humiliating?

The Universal Declaration of Human Rights, that generous declaration with which the United Nations has graced humanity, grants every person the right to work: not only social security and all the other social and economic rights which, in the language of that document, are "indispensable for his dignity" (Article 22), but also the explicit right to work (Article 23).[1] Work is thus not merely a tool for making a dignified living, but a right in and of itself. A society that honors human rights is obligated to provide every person in it with employment even if the person's social rights are guaranteed by unemployment benefits. The right to work granted by that declaration includes the free choice of employment as well as just and decent working conditions.

The question of interest for our purposes is whether work is really a vital condition for human dignity, which cannot be taken away from people who want to work without degrading them. A more up-to-date version of this question is the following. Suppose there is a developed society in which the unemployment rate permanently hovers around the 10 percent mark. Unemployment benefits are paid, however, and the unemployed have the chance of finding odd jobs that supplement their benefits, so that their total income matches that of unskilled workers in the economy. Should we deny this society the status of a decent society because the social arrangements accept the humiliating situation of lack of employment (as defined by the Universal Declaration of Human Rights)? Can a society be considered a decent one only if it has full employment, or at worst temporary unemployment?

When people discuss the high value of work they often speak in a sermonizing tone. It is hard to argue with sermons, but the value of work must be examined from the viewpoint of the workers rather than that of the preachers. The workers' own view of the value of work is not always flattering. Workers may consider work to be of high value, but not every sort of work. Most manual laborers do not want their children to follow in their footsteps. Many workers consider their vacations their best days. They consider their days off to be a more authentic expression of their being than their workdays. It is also true that many of them hate being involuntarily unemployed and feel miserable in such a situation. But it is important to understand why. Are they miserable because of losing their income and their social standing, or because they feel they have lost something of central value in their lives—a way of expressing themselves as human beings, the sort of value artists attach to their work?

I am claiming that people consider their work valuable when it enables them to support themselves through their own labor without being dependent on the goodwill of others. Work gives people the autonomy and economic citizenship that preserves their human dignity. This claim is, of course, culture- and time-dependent. In ancient Greece and Rome hired laborers were considered unworthy of being citizens because they were dependent on their pay. Hired workers were the opposite of gentlemen of independent means. The only people inferior to hired workers were slaves, whose labor was not considered work, in the same sense that military service or homemaking, no matter how hard and wearying, is not considered work.

We are not concerned here with the history of the concept of work, but this history is important in that it reminds us how much people's attitude toward work depends on culture. I mention Greece and Rome in order to point out that the idea of independence we associate with work, even if it is hired labor, is a relatively recent notion. Hired labor was considered undignified in the past partly because the laborer's existence depended on getting paid by others. The present topic is the value of work in developed industrial societies, not in medieval guild societies. In the latter there were undoubtedly artisans like Romain Rolland's carpenter Colas Breugnon whose attitude toward their work was like that of present-day artists. We are discussing the attitude toward work in societies where there is a ramified division of labor. In such societies workers are kept apart from the product of their labor, and this separation is a central factor in the estrangement of workers in modern society.

It is worth distinguishing among four types of dependence that determine people's attitude toward work. The classic notion is dependence on getting paid. The opposite of dependence on pay is autarchic production, in which the producing person does not need anyone else to pay her. Slaves are the ultimate case of dependent labor, since they work by command and their dependence is absolute.

The capitalist concept of dependence is that dependent people are those who are supported by others on a regular basis, when this support is not a remuneration for work or merchandise or property. According to this concept of dependence, work is a means of liberating anyone who does not own property (that is, anyone who has no possibility of existing without depending on others). Unemployment creates dependence, and thus work, like property, liberates one from relying on the kindness of strangers.

The socialist concept of dependence is based on the belief that work is the source of all economic value. Therefore anyone who does not work is parasitically dependent on the work of others. Only the value-producing worker is free of parasitic dependence and thus truly independent.

There is also a Calvinist concept of dependence, in which the only acceptable form of dependence is Man's dependence on God as His servant. Man's work is divine service. Idleness is the neglect of one's holy work, and being dependent on another human being is considered a grievous sin.

Here we have four concepts of dependence embedded in heavily laden doctrines and historical trends. Yet none of these concepts seems to me capable of justifying the value of work. In modern society everyone is dependent on everyone else and there is no place for the notion of autarchy in its classical version. The socialist concept of dependence is based on a theory of the value of work in which the value of any product or service depends in the final analysis on the work incorporated in it. But even if this last argument is refined, it remains false: just consider the price of diamonds.[2] (There is an element of this theory that is correct—the element dealing with the association between work and exploitation. This is discussed in the next section.) The Calvinist concept of work as divine service requires us to accept the existence of God and thus conflicts with the humanistic constraint we have taken upon ourselves. We are left with the capitalist concept— that working for pay liberates the worker from dependence on the generosity of others or on crime. This concept purports to be of great moral significance, since the only way propertyless people can secure their human dignity is by working for pay. But in the final analysis the independence guaranteed by work does not give work a value of its own. There is a better way of being independent in the capitalist view—owning property.

The question we started out with, about the decent

society and its attitude toward unemployment, intentionally severed the tie between work and income. This was done by assuming unemployment benefits, which are meant to guarantee an income even without work. It is important, however, to avoid the fallacy of composition here: the fact that it is possible to provide unemployment benefits to anyone does not imply that it is possible to provide these benefits to everyone or even to a large number of people in the long run. Long-term mass unemployment would drain the resources from which the benefits are paid. The association between work and income still exists, even if only on the aggregate level. A decent society must protect its members against mass unemployment, as otherwise it will no longer be capable of guaranteeing the unemployed an income which can prevent them from sinking into degrading poverty.

But the central question still remains: Must a society guarantee employment to whoever wants it in order to be considered a decent one? One argument in favor of making employment and not only income a condition of the decent society is grounded in Man's nature as a working creature (Homo Faber). The argument is based on the premise that human nature is such as to find its unique expression in work. The humanity of persons is not expressed in all its uniqueness when they are rational in the sense of gazing speculatively at the universe and contemplating eternal truths, but in doing productive work. A society that permits involuntary unemployment thus denies the humanity of the unemployed. Such denial is rejection, and rejection is humiliation. Therefore such a society is not a decent one.

The Homo Faber argument is based on a familiar move

used in defining essences. According to this move working is the unique essence of humans, and the more a person actualizes his essence, the more human he is. My response to this argument is based on a distinction. There is a difference between employment and a meaningful occupation—that is, an occupation that confers meaning on the life of the one engaged in it. Employment may secure income, but it does not guarantee a meaningful occupation. There is no need for a metaphysical justification based on defining the essence of human nature for demanding that a decent society satisfy the difficult but just requirement of guaranteeing all adults an occupation they would consider meaningful—not only one that would grant them self-esteem but one that would give them self-worth. The society is not obliged to afford everyone the occupation that is most meaningful for them, but it is obliged to make a serious attempt to provide some sort of occupation they could consider meaningful, or at least to help them find such an occupation.

It is certainly wrong for a decent society to hinder anyone from attaining a meaningful occupation. But the duty is not merely negative; there is also a positive obligation. A decent society is not obliged to provide employment for the purpose of a livelihood if it has other means of guaranteeing a minimum income, but it is obligated to give each of its members the opportunity to find a reasonably meaningful occupation, such as studying. The meaning of the occupation is subjective, while the requirement of reasonableness is intended to impose constraints that take one's abilities into consideration. An occupation does not necessarily constitute employment in the sense that the meaningful occupation is also the source of income. What provides the person with a meaningful occupation may actually be a hobby. A decent society is thus one that provides all its members with the opportunity to find at least one reasonably meaningful occupation.

Exploitation and Coercion in the Workplace

Here we have two questions to deal with: Is the decent society one in which there is no exploitation? And is it one in which there is no forced labor?

We must distinguish between two meanings of the term "forced labor": work performed under coercion and work performed under compulsion. I am making this distinction following Jon Elster's distinction between coercion and force. According to Elster, coercion requires a person coercing someone else with intention, while force does not require a person doing the forcing, or any intention to force someone to do something. Since the term "forced labor" may be used for both of these senses, I am calling the first one "work under coercion" or "coerced labor," while the second will be called "work under compulsion" or "compulsory labor."

When Palestinian Arabs driving their cars in the occupied territories are arbitrarily stopped and forced to clear away roadblocks placed there by other Arabs, this is humiliating coercion. But if the same Arabs clear away the same roadblocks because they are compelled to support themselves this way, this does not constitute humiliation in and of itself.

Exploiting workers does not necessary mean coercing them to work. Obviously work under coercion is a paradigmatic form of exploitation. Under this rubric I include hard labor in prisons, as long as it is purposeful work making products for the use of people other than the prisoners themselves. The coerced labor of slaves, serfs, or workers impressed into government service is absolutely irreconcilable with a decent society.

But is coerced labor humiliating? At first this seems as strange a question as "What's wrong with acting wrongly?" Work under coercion is a paradigmatic example of humiliation. Someone who is coerced to work is subject to humiliation. But while it would be ridiculous to ask what it is about work under coercion that makes it unfree—where the answer is the coercion—cocrcion and humiliation are not correlated by definition. In coerced labor the victim is physically subordinated to the will of another, and such subordination is a central characteristic of humiliation because it involves taking away the victim's autonomy and control.

Work under coercion is a clear case of humiliation. But coerced labor in the form of slavery, serfdom, or corvée is unlikely to exist in societies that are candidates for being decent societies in our world, while exploitation does exist in such societies. The question is whether it is essential to eradicate all exploitation within a society as a necessary condition for it to be considered a decent one. It was an important argument of Marx's that for exploitation to exist it must be well disguised, for if it were not, the victims would rise up against their exploiters. Exploitation is not a conspiracy of exploiters against their victims. The fact of exploitation is usually hidden from the exploiters as well. In feudal societies, where the coercive element of work was obvious to everyone, the aspect of exploitation was masked by describing the nature of the relationship between the lord and the serfs as one of intimate protection between neighbors, in which the lord provided the protection and the serfs provided products: "I am not enslaved—I work your fields while you go out to protect both of us." In capitalist societies there is no pretense of the supposed intimacy of neighbors.[3] The relationship between the owners of the means of production and the workers is disguised instead as a relationship of mutual benefit between adults in a contractual association, in which the workers provide their labor and skill while the owners of the capital provide the means of production.

There is enough truth in the capitalist picture, just as there is enough truth in the feudal picture, to disguise the exploitative nature of these relationships. I would add that there is also enough truth in the partnership of husband and wife in raising a family to disguise the exploitation of women's work within the family. The question for our purposes is whether exploitation is humiliating: not whether it is unfair, but whether it is humiliating.

Imagine that you are a weaver. You are compelled to work in weaving because you have not been offered any other sort of work. Weaving is the work you know and, perhaps more important, you have to support yourself and your family. This is the sense in which you are compelled to work on the loom. Your employer has only one loom, and she does not know what you too do not know—that the loom was actually stolen from your family in the past. You get only a fraction of what you produce; the rest goes to your employer. One day you find out that you have been compelled to work on a loom which really ought to be yours, and that the person who enjoys the lion's share of what you produce may be the legal owner of the loom, but not its moral owner. You feel exploited. But should you also feel humiliated?

Let me offer a few clarifying remarks about the story of the loom. I am of the opinion put forward by Gerald Cohen, that there is no exploitation without the assumption that on some level or another the means of production which constitutes the capital owner's contribution has been stolen. Not that it has been stolen in the sense of taking property from its legal owner, but in the sense of taking something without the permission of the person who is morally the owner of the property. This concept of moral ownership does not seem strange or problematic to me. The present question is not whether the property has been stolen, however, but whether being employed by the present owner of the stolen property, and paying him for the use of this property, is a sound reason for feeling humiliated.

Imagine now that the person who took over the loom that was supposed to be yours has also taken over many other looms, and with great ingenuity has organized the production of the textiles so that she is able to pay you a salary much higher than the profit you would make from the loom if you were working on it as its owner. Under these circumstances, would you still be justified in feeling exploited?

Three possible responses to this question suggest themselves:

1. You are justified in feeling exploited. Exploitation is a comparative concept. An existing situation is compared with a counterfactual situation. You are justified in saying that if you had gotten together with the

rightful owners of the other stolen looms you could have earned more than what your employer, the loom thief, is paying you. The relevant comparison according to this approach is not how much you would have earned as the owner of a lone loom, but how much you could have earned by properly organizing the work with people sharing your interests.

2. You should indeed compare what you are earning now with what you could have earned as owner of the loom. However, you have no right to compare it with what you could have earned if you had organized the work in a way that neither you nor others would ever actually have done. Your employer has made a real contribution to production, and you have no right to consider yourself exploited. You do have the right to feel bad in a situation in which you are working as an employee on a loom which should really be yours. But if exploitation means not receiving a fair recompense in terms of the produced value, then you do not have the right to consider yourself exploited.

3. If the loom was clearly and directly stolen from you, then it is entirely obvious that you are the injured party. The only thing left to be determined is whether the remuneration you have received is sufficient to compensate for the damages. One of the things that must be included in the compensation is the recognition that it serves as a compensation. Our case involves ownership and theft hidden from the actors, and requires historical and "scientific" detective work to discover that the loom actually belongs to you. Meanwhile, you realize that the reparation you have received in virtue of the fact that the loom was not in

your possession is actually more than what you could have received on your own. In this case, then, you do not have a good reason for feeling exploited. Only bitterness based on envy could lead you to feel exploited. Not only do you have no right to consider yourself deprived, you should even consider yourself lucky.

One might argue against this that even in the last case there is reason to feel exploited, since your autonomy has been diminished by the fact that the loom was taken from you, even if your income has increased. Your autonomy includes the right to act foolishly, that is, to earn less than you would if you worked for someone else. Let me explain. The right to act unwisely is an important component of the concept of autonomy. In other words, autonomy includes the right to make wrong decisions, even with the most painful results, and to bear the responsibility for the outcome. It is entirely possible that if your life were run paternalistically by someone wiser than you who has your best interests at heart—say, your father or mother—you would make fewer mistakes in such enterprises as choosing a marriage partner. But if someone else made your decisions for you, this would drastically diminish your autonomy, demoting you to the level of a nonadult human being. This is liable to be humiliating even if your loving parent had no intention of humiliating you.

This is the way things are for an individual, and the issue of autonomy is much the same for encompassing groups as well. Thus, for example, it may turn out that colonial rule in certain countries organized production in such a way that their output was much greater than it would have been if the colonies had been on their own. Moreover, when the colonial rule was overthrown, production in most of the colonies greatly decreased. Yet we would still want to say that the colonial regime diminished the autonomy of the societies it ruled over, and thus indirectly diminished the autonomy of their members as well. Do we also want to say that these countries were exploited by the colonial regime? This depends in part on such questions as whether the colonial regime exploited irreplaceable raw materials in these countries. It is entirely possible to apply to colonial rule what I am inclined to say about the case in which I am earning more than I would if the loom belonged to me. There is no exploitation here, but there may be humiliation, since colonies under such rule have their autonomy impaired.

The central question still remains to be answered: Is there an inherent connection between exploitation and humiliation? My answer is no. Exploitation based on compulsion that is not coercion is not necessarily humiliating. Exploitation is not just and it is not fair, but it is does not necessarily imply a lack of decency. The side effects of exploitation are liable to be humiliating, but the act of exploitation itself does not constitute humiliation. It does not fit the sense of humiliation as rejection from the human race, nor does it fit the sense of a fatal blow to the individual's autonomy in which he or she is stripped of basic control. Producing goods on equipment that should have been yours is not humiliating in and of itself. Only if the means of production were explicitly stolen from you, and you are coerced to work on them, can we say that humiliation is added to injury. This is the humiliation that results from coercion, and from helplessness in the face of the robber who has turned into a protector. If the Mafia coerces you as the owner of a restaurant to pay protection money, but guarantees you a crowd of customers which increases your income even after the protection money is deducted, you are still humiliated because you are under a terrorizing, coercive protection racket. You are not exploited, but you are humiliated. The connection between exploitation and humiliation is causal rather than conceptual. Therefore a society may be decent even though it is exploitative.

16

Punishment

Punishment is the litmus test of the decent society. The way a society conducts its punishment policies and procedures puts it to the test of whether or not it is a decent society. The respect that must be accorded criminals is basic human respect; they clearly must not be granted any social honor. Thus looking at punishment is a good way of examining whether a society is decent and treats human beings as human. The paradigm case of punishment is imprisonment, so this will be the main focus of our discussion.

We have a simple formula which claims that a society is a decent one if it punishes its criminals—even the worst of them—without humiliating them. After all, a criminal is a human being. Every human being, even a criminal, is entitled to the respect granted to humans because they are human. An injury to human dignity is humiliation, and so even a criminal is entitled not to be humiliated. A decent society must not provide sound reasons for criminals to consider their dignity violated, even if their punishment gives them good reason to consider their social honor impaired (although perhaps with habitual criminals the reference group is located within the prison walls, and it is precisely there that they may receive their social honor).

The central question of this section is whether efficient yet nonhumiliating punishment is possible, where efficiency is determined by the society's success in maintaining order through the punishment—that is, through deterrence—or whether requiring the decent society to avoid humiliating its prisoners is a utopian demand that would endanger its existence.

Foucault stressed the ritualistic nature of punishment in premodern societies.[1] Extreme physical torture was inflicted in elaborate rituals, in which the criminal was put to a slow death in a thousand and one unnatural ways. The amount of pain inflicted was carefully calculated, where the principle of making the punishment fit the crime was often distorted to a disproportionate punishment that might be called "an eye for a tooth." The punishment had a public, theatrical nature, featuring the torture wheel, the stake, the gallows, and dragging the bound victim through the city streets—all of which were intended to inflict the tortures of Hell on the condemned person before actually killing him.

The profound cruelty of this form of punishment was also intended to humiliate the victim. Of course, the person who was being punished by this sort of physical torture scarcely cared about the loss of his human dignity. But the ceremony was intended for the spectators, and its degrading intent often had the opposite effect on them. The spectators often responded to these show punishments by identifying with the victim and becoming enraged at the torturing and humiliating regime.[2] The humiliation became the focus for elevating the victim in the spectators' eyes, as if the tortures had cleansed the victim of his sins.

Ceremonial punishment involves not only torture but also symbolic gestures. The role of symbols in punishment is an important one, but it should not be mistaken for the main role, which was played by physical cruelty. Mutilating the criminal's body, such as by cutting off a hand, is undoubtedly a humiliating act, but it is first of all physically painful and injurious. When King David cut off the hands and feet of Rechab and Baanah (II Samuel 4:12), and when Adoni-bezek cut off the thumbs and big toes of the seventy kings who picked up scraps under his table (Judges 1:7), they intended to humiliate their enemies into the ground. But we must remember that physical cruelty takes precedence over humiliation. Torturing the body causes more acute pain than torturing the soul. The decent society is based on the principle of eliminating humiliation, but it presupposes that physical cruelty has already been eradicated.

George Bernard Shaw considered old-fashioned punishment less humiliating than the modern sort, because the old-fashioned kind presented the victims' suffering publicly rather than concealing it. Modern punishment, in contrast, hides criminals from the public eye, thus preventing others from sharing their pain. Indifference to people's suffering means rejecting them from human society. It is therefore important to distinguish between cruelty and humiliation, since the central factor in old-fashioned punishment was cruelty, whereas we are concerned with the humiliating aspect of punishment.

There is another prefatory note to the issue of the

decent society's attitude to punishment—again inspired by Foucault—which is needed to serve as a warning sign. This is the fact that the demand for humane punishment has historically been motivated by something more than a newly acquired sensitivity to human suffering. The punishment reforms based on the demand to treat criminals humanely have stemmed from changes in the economics of punishment. On the one hand, the old regime behaved especially violently and savagely toward condemned prisoners, yet, on the other, it had a high tolerance for illegality. This tolerance was associated not only with the special privileges of the nobility but also with lenient treatment of illegal behavior on the part of the lower classes, derived from a nonmoralistic attitude to their criminality. The rise of the bourgeoisie and their business requirements created the need to take punitive steps to protect property and businesses efficiently. It therefore became necessary for lawbreakers to be punished broadly and uniformly.

Thus there was, on the one hand, a demand to restrict barbaric types of punishment and, on the other, a demand to extend the areas in which lawbreaking was punished. It was not only changing moral sensitivities that changed people's attitude toward punishment, but also, and perhaps even primarily, responsiveness to the needs of the economy and the society. These changes were often masked by the assumption of a "humane" attitude, but we must be careful not to ideologize the historical notion of humane punishment. Yet, even if Foucault is right and the motives for "humane" punishment were not particularly noble ones, this should not affect our demand that the decent society justify itself by appealing to human dignity as a central value, rather than by safeguarding the interests of a respectable society that is not necessarily a decent one. In other words, our specific interest in the punishment policies of the decent society is based on the idea that these policies should be carefully constrained by regard for human dignity.

Punishment and Humiliation

There is no internal relation between medical treatment and causing pain. Most medicine may be bitter, but there is no reason in principle that medicine could not be sweeter than wine. The notion that if the disease is as bitter as gall the cure must be so as well is a magical notion, not a medical one. In contrast, there is an internal relation between punishment and causing suffering, where suffering also includes mental anguish. There are, to be sure, stories like the one by O. Henry about the man who did everything he could to be thrown into jail on a cold winter day in order to get some hot soup. Such a case, however, does not refute the claim that there is an internal relation between punishment and suffering, since in that case being in prison was not a punishment but a relief.

Implementing a systematic policy of causing suffering is not evidence of humiliation in and of itself. Many armies have the policy of causing suffering to recruits in combat units with the intention of toughening but not necessarily humiliating them. Recruits, like prisoners, have their freedom taken away. Recruits are given orders that are often harsher than those given to criminals in prison, but recruits should not be subject to the element of disgrace that exists in the treatment of prisoners. Punishing prisoners is intended to make them feel disgraced, that is, to shame and dishonor them. The emphasis here is still on social honor. If disgrace is taken to the extreme, however, it may become injury to human dignity, which is humiliation. This is not true of the normative treatment of recruits. The law distinguishes between punishments that do or do not involve disgrace, but the sort of punishment we are concerned with here is the kind that does involve disgrace. Although recruits are often subject to humiliating treatment on the part of their commanding officers, this humiliation is not a built-in element of the institution of basic training.

Our question, then, is whether the humiliating element can be eliminated from the punishment of prisoners. On the one hand there is the claim that any punishment which inherently involves suffering and disgrace is necessarily humiliating. The humiliating element may be mitigated, but if the imprisonment has some purpose it cannot be achieved without the suffering and humiliation involved in keeping the prisoner away from human society. On the other hand there is the claim that it is precisely punishment, with all the suffering it involves, which acknowledges that the person being punished is punishable—that is, a moral agent—and therefore worthy of respect. If, however, someone is taken out of the category of the punishable and placed in the category of patient—because, say, she is mentally ill and so not responsible for her actions—then no disgrace is attached to her behavior, but she is removed from the class of beings worthy of respect as moral agents. The honor of being punishable sounds like an oxymoron, while Hegel's praise of punishment as based on the right of the criminal to be punished sounds altogether macabre. But consider recruits in boot camp who are cursing the day they were born. There is nothing ironic about saying that these recruits, and certainly outside spectators who identify with the army's goals, consider their service an honor and a privilege rather than merely a burdensome duty.

We are thus faced with two conflicting claims. The first one states that punishment is inherently humiliating. The second claim is that the very fact that criminals are punished shows that they are being taken seriously as human beings. This fact attests to their being basically respected, and is no more ironic than the claim that army recruits are respected for the very fact that they are being trained for elite army service.

We must not allow ourselves to be caught between the two horns of this dilemma. It is possible to think about punishment without any inherent association with humiliation. The idea is that the model for nonhumiliating punishment must be the model of basic training at its best. Both recruits and prisoners are at the bottom of the social hierarchy in the army and in society respectively. Both basic training and imprisonment are unpleasant situations involving lack of privacy, constant supervision, and absolute lack of autonomy—in other words, they are situations with the potential for being humiliating. And just as society is not interested in humiliating recruits, seeing them rather from a nonhumiliating point of view, so must we treat prisoners who are being punished. In practice, of course, both recruits and prisoners are often humiliated. Recruits are humiliated in the role of liminal social beings undergoing the initiation rite that is basic training. Prisoners, in contrast, are humiliated in the role of marginal beings—that is, they are rejected from human society.

An appalling element in both situations—basic training as well as imprisonment—is the fact that recruits and prisoners are often humiliated by their fellow inmates. Humiliation by fellow inmates occurs under the responsibility of the institution, since both the army and the prisons are total institutions. Therefore humiliation by fellow inmates counts as institutional humiliation.

The idea that society's attitude toward army recruits is the model for the decent society's attitude to prisoners is a problematic one. Punishment is also a communicative act intended to give both the society and the criminal the message that crime is associated with disgrace. There is no analogous communicative act with respect to recruits. On the contrary, the message communicated to recruits is that they have the right to be proud of what they are undergoing, even if it is harsh, or perhaps especially because it is harsh. Since the communicative acts are different in the two situations, the punishment of imprisonment is rightly interpreted as involving disgrace, while this is an unacceptable interpretation of the significance of basic training. The claim that punishment is a communicative act is a statement of fact and should not be construed as support for any particular view about the purpose of punishment—whether it is seen as a deterrent, or a form of rehabilitation, or ensuring that justice is done, or even revenge. All these justifications for punishment require it to communicate the idea that crime involves disgrace. The question is how to transform the idea of the disgrace inherent in punishment into a concept involving only the loss of social honor without personal humiliation as well.

In other words, how can we transform prisoners into civilian "recruits," which would mean not rejecting the prisoners from human society?

This is a difficult practical question, but not a difficult conceptual one. A decent society cares about the dignity of its prisoners.

Conclusion

The first three parts of this book dealt with the question of what constitutes a decent society. The fourth part dealt with the issue of how to apply the idea of a decent society to various areas of life, such as employment and punishment. These concluding remarks, which are not a summary, attempt the important task of comparing the decent society with the just society. The comparison involves both content and method.

First let us try to understand what a just society is, in the light of John Rawls's famous theory of justice. Is it possible to have a just society that is not a decent society? In other words, can a society be founded on justice, yet contain humiliating institutions? Is it possible for a just society, as defined by Rawls, not to be a decent one? My focus on Rawls's concept of a just society is not meant to obscure the existence of other concepts of justice that are worthy of comparison with the decent society. My exclusive reference to Rawls's notion of justice plays a limited role here—namely, to indicate that, although it seems obvious that a just society must also be a decent one, it is not as obvious as it seems. Put differently, it is correct to

271

say that a just society must be a decent society, but it is not obviously correct. Indeed, my discussion of Rawls's concept of justice is meant to attest that the connection between the two types of society is not obvious. The idea is that if a theory with "Kantian" sensitivity to human dignity such as Rawls's is liable to encounter difficulties in reconciling the just and the decent society, then the relation between the two types of society is less clear than it might seem.

According to Rawls, a just society is based on two principles of justice:

A. Each person has an equal right to the most extensive scheme of equal basic liberties compatible with similar schemes for all.
B. Social or economic inequalities must satisfy two conditions: (1) they must benefit the least advantaged members of the society; and (2) they must be attached to offices and positions open to all under conditions of fair and equal opportunity.[1]

The question thus is whether a society based on Rawls's principles of justice is logically reconcilable with the existence of humiliating institutions. There is no doubt that the spirit of the just society, based on the two principles of liberty and justified difference, conflicts essentially with a nondecent society. But one can still ask whether a Rawls-style just society conflicts in the letter, and not only in the spirit, with a society that contains humiliating institutions.

Rawls's just society is concerned with the just distribution of primary goods. These are goods that all rational individuals are expected to want irrespective of anything else they may want—they want these goods for their own sake. These primary goods include basic liberties such as freedom of speech and conscience, freedom of movement and choice of career, along with income and capital. The primary good that is prior to all these is self-respect. In Rawls's view, self-respect has two aspects: the sense people have of themselves based on their own value, and the sense that their life plan is worthy of realization, accompanied by the confidence that they have the ability to carry out this plan, as far as it is up to them.

Why is self-respect the most basic primary good? Because without self-respect there is no point in doing anything whatsoever. Without self-respect one has no sense of value or any sense that life has meaning: "Vanity of vanities, all is vanity." Rational people who want to establish a just society will do everything they can to avoid creating humiliating institutions or social conditions, since these would diminish the most basic primary good of self-respect. Moreover, while Rawls's principle of difference determines under which conditions it is acceptable to deviate from equal distribution for primary goods consisting of material wealth, there is no room for any inequality in the distribution of self-respect.

It doesn't matter here that Rawls's concept of self-respect is not the same as mine. It is clear that the spirit of a just society cannot tolerate systematic humiliation by its basic institutions. This is especially true since the good to be distributed, in the form of social conditions that enable people to have self-respect, is at the top of the just society's priority list. If humiliation means damaging people's self-respect, then it is clear that a necessary condition for the just society is that it should be a society that does not humiliate its members.

But what about the possibility of institutional humiliation in a society that is just to its members, but not to
others? Kibbutz society in Israel is an outstanding example of a society that heroically attempted in its heyday to
construct a just society for its members, but has always
been insensitive to nonmembers, such as hired workers
from outside the kibbutz. Kibbutz society might not be
Rawlsian society, but it serves to indicate the problems
involved in a society which is just to its own members, but
not to those dependent on it who are not its members.
For Rawls the just society is founded on a contract among
its members, which guarantees just institutions for the
partners to the contract. Even those with the most inferior
positions in the just society are still considered members
of the society. But the worst problems of humiliation in
the modern world are often those of people who are not
members of the society they live in—people who do not
belong.[2] Perhaps the least advantaged people in the
United States today are the illegal Mexican immigrants
whose lack of a work license turns them into serfs, if not
degraded slaves, of the employers who keep them and
hide them. These Mexicans are not members of society.
They are not American citizens, and they are not taken
into account when considering who is the least advantaged in American society.

The kibbutz example suggests that a commitment to
justice among members does not ensure a decent society.
Kibbutz society in its finest hours was the closest approximation I know of to a society that tried to be just to its
members, but it was not a decent society. Many people
who had to deal with the kibbutz but did not belong to it
often felt humiliated by it, and justifiably. In order to

assess whether a Rawlsian just society is also decent, it must therefore be judged by its treatment of people who are dependent on its institutions even if they are not members, such as foreign workers *(Gastarbeiter)*, who do the dirty work in developed countries without being citizens there. Thus, in order to evaluate the claim that being a decent society is a necessary condition for a Rawlsian just society, we must clarify what Rawls's criteria are for belonging to a society. We especially need to clarify the status of nonmembers in a just society. I am certain that a just society ought, in Rawls's view, to be a decent society in spirit, both to members and to nonmembers, but I am not sure how closely the letter follows the spirit.

Aside from the issue of belonging to the society, there is another problem that needs to be clarified before we can determine whether a Rawlsian just society is necessarily also a decent society. Rawls's just society is concerned with establishing rules for the society's basic institutions. When Rawls gives an example of what he considers nonbasic institutions that he does not intend to discuss, he mentions religious rituals. But where the decent society is concerned, rituals are actually very important. For example, various religions, and various streams within some religions, exclude women from equal and active participation in religious ritual. Women are generally excluded from officiating at ceremonies and from participating in central aspects of the ceremonies. Some religious groups have begun to demand women's full and equal participation in rituals. Excluding women from religious ritual means denying them the status of full membership in an encompassing group that is very important in their lives. It does not mean rejecting women as nonhuman, but it does mean denying their status as adult human beings. If the reason that Halakha—Jewish law—does not permit women to read from the Torah scroll before a congregation including men is "for the sake of the honor of the congregation," then it is clear that women's human honor is not the same as that of men.

It is important, however, to be precise about what the exclusion of women from certain religious ceremonies actually tells us about how their status is perceived. Not every act of exclusion is an act of rejection. In Jewish ritual there are ceremonies such as the priestly blessing where only men considered to be descendants of the priestly caste are allowed to give the blessing. Ordinary Jews who are not members of this caste do not view themselves as humiliated or insulted or embarrassed purely in virtue of the fact that they do not belong to the group of men who are halakhically permitted to give the priestly blessing. But the reason for this is simple: being a member of the priestly caste has no significance nowadays in Jewish community life. In contrast, the exclusion of women from religious ceremonies or from certain aspects of these ceremonies is highly significant in community life. This is manifested, for example, in the fact that only the males in this community are obligated to study the Torah, and in a serious sense only they are obligated to pray regularly. The division of labor between men and women is such that the women do not share fully in the performance of the commandments and ritual obligations, and hence are not full members of the community.

The problem here is not whether a decent society would act differently than a just society in allowing women to participate in rituals. The question is whether Rawls's concept of the just society is at all concerned with religious ritual as a social institution, or whether this institution is not considered sufficiently basic to be counted in evaluating a just society. A decent society is judged in part by institutions such as religious ritual. Our discussion of institutions is in general on a lower level of abstraction than Rawls's principled discussion. The question thus is not what to do about the discrimination against women in religious ritual. The present question is whether religious ritual is considered within the range of institutions to be judged and evaluated in a general evaluation of societies as decent ones, in contrast to their evaluation as just ones. Here we may find a difference between the range of application of the discussion in the case of the Rawlsian just society and in the case of our own decent society.

An important element in our account of the concept of the decent society involves the status of encompassing groups within the society. Belonging to an encompassing group is one way that people give their life meaning. Rejection from a legitimate encompassing group—and, as a rule, belonging to religious groups is legitimate—is thus liable to be a humiliating act. In this book I have focused on the humiliation of encompassing groups by the institutions of the society. I have hardly discussed the humiliation of people within the encompassing groups they belong to. An encompassing group is a mediating element between the individual and the general society. Such groups are meant to support and elevate the individual, but they may turn out in practice to be oppressive and humiliating. Although I restricted the encompassing groups to legitimate ones, I did not specify in detail the constraints that determine whether a given encompassing group is legitimate or not. For example, it is not clear whether its institutions have the right to humiliate their deviant members.

One might argue that belonging to an encompassing group within a society is nothing more than voluntarily joining a group. Any individual may have to decide whether he wants to belong to an encompassing group that is liable to punish him in a humiliating way, such as by throwing him out, if he deviates from its norms. Thus it is not necessary to place any restrictions on these voluntary encompassing groups in order for the society to be considered a decent one, just as there is no need to forbid humiliating treatment, even of the worst sort, between a sadist and a masochist, as long as the individuals involved are consenting adults.

It would be grossly unrealistic to portray an individual's belonging to an encompassing group of significance in his life, such as a religion or nationality, as if it were a free contractual connection with other consenting adults. The reason encompassing groups have such power in the life of individuals is precisely that they are not corporations in a market economy toward which one can have a "take it or leave it" attitude. This important fact may lead the encompassing group to act tyrannically toward its members, who are so greatly dependent on it. When we evaluate the behavior of social institutions in order to determine whether they are humiliating, we must also include the behavior of the institutions and organizations of the encompassing groups in the society. If we see that the voluntary nature of these organizations is doubtful, and it is not easy to be accepted into other significant encompassing groups, then humiliating behavior on the part of these institutions taints the entire society. In such a case, a decent society must offer itself as a desirable alternative to any encompassing group within it, so that individuals can identify with it and build a satisfying way of life within the larger society. At any rate, a decent society is judged not only on the basis of whether its institutions treat encompassing groups in a humiliating way but also on the basis of how the institutions of the encompassing groups treat their own members. The issue for discussion here is no less than the legitimacy of encompassing groups, which is partly dependent on these groups' treating their members in a nonhumiliating way.

Following Albert Hirschman, we can distinguish between two dimensions of evaluation of encompassing groups.[3] One is the dimension of "voice"—the price an individual in the group pays for criticizing its institutions and members. The second dimension is "exit"—the price the individual pays for leaving the group. Encompassing groups are oppressive when both sorts of price are high. This is the case when the price of "voice" or "exit" is humiliation.

Let us return to the relationship between the decent society and the just society. Rawls distinguishes between two aspects involved in cutting the economic cake. One is the *pattern* of just distribution—for example, equal portions for all. The other is the *procedure* used to obtain the just distribution—for example, the person who cuts the cake gets her piece last. This way we can ensure that it will be in her own interest to cut the cake into equal portions.

Rawls defines perfect procedural justice as a case in which there is a just pattern of distribution according to some criterion external to the distributional procedures. Procedures are perfectly just if they efficiently give rise to a just distribution according to a just distributive pattern. Rawls distinguishes this from imperfect procedural justice, which he defines as a situation in which the distributive procedures have a high probability of giving rise to a just pattern of distribution, but certainty is lacking. Rawls claims that only imperfect procedural justice can exist in the real world.

But the way distributors act should also be examined. The people distributing the goods may act in a humiliating way even if the end result is the best possible distribution of the goods. Thus, for example, I have claimed that even if a charity society provided the same distribution of goods as a welfare society, there could remain a crucial difference between them if the goods were distributed in the former with an attitude of pity toward the recipients, while in the latter they were distributed with the recognition of the recipients' right to obtain them. We might, for instance, see people distributing food to famine victims in Ethiopia throw the food out of the truck as if the recipients were dogs, while still making sure that all the recipients get their just portion in an efficient manner. Efficiency, we recall, involves only the probability of obtaining a just pattern of distribution, and not a humane manner of distribution. The distribution may be both efficient and just, yet still humiliating.

The claim that there can be bad manners in a just society may seem petty—confusing the major issue of ethics with the minor one of etiquette. But it is not petty. It reflects an old fear that justice may lack compassion and might even be an expression of vindictiveness. There is a suspicion that the just society may become mired in rigid calculations of what is just, which may replace gentleness and humane consideration in simple human relations. The requirement that a just society should also be a decent one means that it is not enough for goods to be distributed justly and efficiently—the style of their distribution must also be taken into account.

So far I have mentioned some strictures against the claim that a (Rawlsian) just society is necessarily also a decent society. We have seen that one stricture relates to the issue of membership in a just society, another relates to the range of the institutions to be judged as just or unjust, and a third to the possibility that a distribution may be procedurally humiliating in spite of being inherently just. None of these strictures questions the basic fact that the just society, as defined by Rawls, is decidedly a decent society in spirit. The question is only whether the Rawlsian just society is also necessarily a decent society according to the letter—that is, according to Rawls's actual formulations. Here the response, based on the three criticisms mentioned, is that at best the answer to this question is unclear, while in the worst case it is possible for a Rawlsian just society not to be a decent society, which is not a tolerable consequence for a just society.

Ideals and Strategies

Is a decent society a necessary stop on the way to realizing a just society? Is it a temporary ideal on the path to the fulfillment of the supreme social ideal of a just society? Irrespective of the relationship between the decent society and the Rawlsian just society, it would seem that being decent is one of the criteria that a just society must fulfill. A separate question is whether a decent society must actually be established on the way to founding a just society in the real political sense. Is there a danger that the decent society will serve as a palliative ersatz for the establishment of a just society? Will the substitution of the less demanding goal of a decent society for the more demanding one of a just society prevent people from striving hard by lowering their aspirations?

My intention in this section is to discuss the notions of the decent and the just society as social ideals. In other words, I would like to look at these notions as regulative ideas rather than evaluative concepts, and explore the relationship between them from this viewpoint.

The dominant political and educational strategy for achieving social and personal ideals is the idealistic strategy. It is based on the presentation of an ideal: whether of a perfect society or of a perfect person whom we are supposed to emulate and approach as best we can. Social and educational doctrines which are polar opposites of one another in the ideals they espouse may often share this idealistic strategy. The term "idealistic strategy" follows the ordinary, everyday use of the word "idealism" in the sense of a determined effort to reach an ideal without considering the obstacles along the way. This strategy is based on an implicit acceptance of the "approximation assumption": if you are striving toward an ideal and you encounter an obstacle on your path, then if you ignore the obstacle you may not achieve the ideal but you'll get to the closest possible approximation to it. This assumption is based on a picture of the ideal as the top of a mountain. If there is something preventing you from reaching the peak, you should try to get as close to the peak as possible.[4]

But the approximation assumption is not always tenable. This was stressed by the economists who developed the so-called theory of the second-best. They came to realize that sometimes, when there is an obstacle to achieving the best (optimal) situation, the proper strategy to use is not the idealistic strategy of ignoring the obstacle. In economic theory the idea has been formulated precisely, but it is easy to recognize it in other areas as well.[5] To illustrate the idea most simply, let us replace the picture of climbing a mountain by a different spatial model. Imagine that you are an amateur pilot and your ideal is to spend a few days on vacation in Hawaii, but you discover that you don't have quite enough fuel in your tank to get there. It would not be a very good idea to attempt to get as close to Hawaii as possible, since you would end up somewhere in the Pacific Ocean. Although you would be as near to Hawaii as you could get, you would be very far from an ideal place to spend your vacation. The alternative strategy is to fly somewhere else, where you have enough fuel in your tank to get to. Try Miami Beach.

St. Paul believed that the human ideal for men is celibacy. But if someone has strong desires, he had better not remain a bachelor, trying to fornicate as little as possible and thus coming as close as possible to the ideal even if he can never actually reach it. It would be better for him to get married. Marriage is second-best to celibacy because it involves giving up the possibility of absolute devotion to the worship of God, which is the best, and which is only possible in a life of chastity. Nevertheless, marriage is still preferable to fornicating bachelorhood.

It is doubtful whether the decent society is a low peak on the mountain ridge that has to be climbed by anyone striding toward the high peak of the just society. It is quite possible that the political strategy for the realization of the decent society is very different from that intended to bring about the just society, even if a just society is necessarily a decent one. A decent society is a worthy ideal to be realized. Its realization does not have to be justified by the claim that it is a necessary step on the way to realizing the just society, especially since it is doubtful whether this last claim is correct. The ideals of the decent and the just society are both optimistic ones, in that they describe a situation which is better than the existing one. Having an optimistic view of an ideal's good features does not necessarily entail being optimistic about the chances of realizing that social ideal. Political conservatism is the view (or the fallacy) that optimistic ideals should not be adopted because there is no reason to be optimistic about the realization of the ideals. I don't think this is reason enough to discredit an ideal. Thus I retain the optimistic ideal of a just society. But I am more optimistic about the chances for establishing a decent society than about the chances for realizing a just society.

A Theory of the Just Society and a Story about a Decent Society

I have avoided presenting my discussion of the decent society under the label of a "theory." The term "theory" is a vague concept. I would like to make a few remarks about the use of this term, especially in connection with the phrase "theory of justice" (in the Rawlsian sense). The point of these remarks is to emphasize the status I attribute to my account of the decent society.

Two mathematical models underlie systems that purport to serve as theories. One model for theories is Hilbertian, the other Gödelian. Let me explain. The Hilbertian model of mathematics is based on the idea that mathematics can be divided into two parts. One part is familiar and understood intuitively. This is the part that includes the finite natural numbers. The other part is understood only in a formal, syntactic sense, through its logical connections with the intuitive part, from which it is derived. This is the model used by the logical positivists, especially Reichenbach and Carnap, to construct their accounts of scientific theories. Every scientific theory worthy of the name thus has two components. One is the observational component, which is understood completely and directly. The second, theoretical, component is understood through rules connecting it with the observational one.

The Gödelian model, which underlies Rawls's theory of justice, is based on Gödel's famous incompleteness theorem. In the proof of this theorem we assume that we have a complete, theory-independent list of all the true statements of arithmetic. In parallel there is a system of axioms (of arithmetic and logic) from which the theorems of arithmetic are derived. The crucial question is whether the collection of theorems that can be logically derived from the given axioms is identical to the list of true statements we assumed to exist at the outset. Gödel's famous answer is that the lists are not identical (he displayed a true sentence which cannot be derived from the axioms).

This Gödelian structure was adopted by Chomsky to

create a theory that purports to be empirical. Chomsky assumes on the one hand that we can generate a complete, theory-independent list of all the sentences of our language that we judge to be grammatical. On the other hand we have a grammar whose rules we use to derive grammatical sentences. We then compare the sentences derived from the grammar with the ones on the list. We decide whether this grammar is an adequate theory of our language on the basis of the extent of the overlap between the sentences derived from the grammar and the sentences on the list that we have intuitively judged to be grammatical. In principle, the grammar is supposed to be adapted to fit the list of intuitive judgments, but it is entirely reasonable to change the direction of fit on occasion. That is, the theory sometimes leads us to change our intuitive judgment in cases where this judgment is inconsistent with other judgments of ours.

Rawls too adopted the Gödelian model of explaining judgments about the just society as a fair society. On the one hand we have intuitive judgments of the fairness of various arrangements for distributing primary goods. On the other hand we have a set of principles (the "theory") from which the judgments about just distribution arrangements are supposed to be derived. In a refined empirical theory the judgments on the theory-independent list have primary status, so that the theory has to fit these judgments. The judgments are the data that the theory is meant to explain. In Rawls's theory, however, there is room for mutual adjustments between the judgments derived from the theory and those arrived at independently. One's intuitions may be guided by one's theory. Rawls called this situation of mutual adjustment "reflective equilibrium."

Rawls adds a new idea to the Gödelian structure of his theory: the theory and the judgments derived from it also serve as arguments for justifying moves in a game-theoretic situation—a situation in which rational players are negotiating the establishment of a constitution for a just society to which they can all agree. The constraint on this "game" of establishing a constitution is that it is unacceptable to use premises containing specific information about the player's position in society in the arguments justifying the constitution. (This is a nonmetaphorical account of Rawls's "veil of ignorance.") This constraint does not mean that the players have to psychologically ignore their possible place in the various social arrangements they are deciding on, but rather that they are expected to act like a judge who hears inadmissible evidence in the course of a trial. The judge may not use this evidence in arriving at a decision. Similarly, Rawls does not allow the participants in the establishment of the constitution to make use of information involving their personal positions. In other words, it is forbidden to justify the constitution with arguments relying on information about the participants' specific characteristics.

There is yet a third important format for theories that we ought to consider, since it is immediately relevant to the present discussion. This is the model of critical theories as formulated by the Frankfurt school. The most prominent examples of this model are the theories of Marx and Freud. These theories have an emancipating, "redemptive" goal—they aim to emancipate people from oppression which is to a considerable degree self-inflicted. Critical theories are actually also theories about judgments: they criticize present judgments, which are considered by the theory to be judgments formed under conditions of oppression, and offer in their place the judgments free people would make. A critical theory is a theory about the judgments of people whom the theory itself is supposed to liberate. It is a reflexive theory which treats itself as subject matter for this very theory. The test of the theory is the willingness of emancipated people to accept it. While the judgments on the independent list are the final arbiters of the truth of a theory in the Gödelian model, and in Rawls's theory there is room for mutual adjustments, when it comes to critical theories the direction of fit is not from the theory to the judgments but vice versa. The judgments are determined by the theory, and they become the independent judgments of people who are free to act in their own true interests.

It might seem that an account of a decent society calls for a critical theory, but I don't think that what I am suggesting in this book is a critical theory, let alone any other kind of theory. I have no theory. I am suggesting a picture of a decent society based partly on an analysis of concepts from the semantic field of respect and humiliation. In analyzing these evaluative concepts I did not keep to the most prevalent uses of these terms in our language. Thus, for example, I am well aware that the most prevalent use of the word "humiliation" is not to describe the rejection of persons from the Family of Man, but rather the lowering of persons from their social status to a "humbler" one. The public demotion of a soldier for misdeeds in army service, as in the case of Dreyfus, is a paradigmatic example of a case where the word "humiliation" would be used. Another prevalent usage of "humiliation" is for the deflation of a person's social aspirations, such as when a candidate who was soundly defeated in an election sees herself as rejected by the voters, although she certainly does not consider herself rejected as a human being.

The sense in which I have used the word "humiliation"—as rejection from the Family of Man—also exists, as I see it, and is often used in cases involving the "demotion" of those who are already at the bottom of the social ladder, so that there is no "lower" place to "demote" them to. Examples are the humiliation of prisoners, army recruits, helpless cripples, the unemployed, and the indigent. The semantic field I am suggesting is not a mere arbitrary decision to attach certain senses to certain terms, yet it is not based on the primary or most prevalent uses of these terms. I am speaking here of explanatory primacy rather than historical primacy. The use of one term is more primary than another if the first is used in explaining the second but not vice versa.

What I am offering here is not a theory but rather a story about the decent society—a story whose heroes are concepts. It is not a medieval-style allegory in which Honor and Humiliation are personified heroes, but a story in which the concepts remain concepts, and the picture obtained is that of a utopia through which to criticize reality.

There is a danger implicit in the concepts used in this book. They are taken from the rhetoric aiming for the sublime that is used in moral and political discourse. The arousing function of concepts such as honor and humiliation is liable to turn discussions of the decent society into a lot of hot air—that is, discussions with no concern for truth but only for the creation of a warm, uplifting atmosphere.[6] Another danger is that the discussion will become mired in a sticky morass of sermonizing, a form of discourse that is not necessarily indifferent to truth, but has no interest in argumentation or in making distinctions. I believe, however, that an intelligent form of discourse is possible which is not theoretical, yet is far from sticky sermonizing or hot air.

The foundational concepts in my work on the decent society, such as respect, humiliation, and the like, are concepts requiring an analysis that goes beyond their sense alone. What is needed in addition is an account of sensibility. When William James attempted to explain the meaning of the concept "or," he said it was the feeling you have when you are at a crossroads and have to decide whether to go left or right. The "or" is the hesitation you feel at the fork in the road. The logical understanding of a concept, in my view, does not require us to feel anything. In the case of "or" it is almost certain that we feel nothing at all. But if we wanted to explain "To be or not to be" not as a logical tautology but as a central existential question, then the emotion and the mood associated with the "or" in the Shakespearean expression would be vital for understanding it. Here a logical understanding of "or" is insufficient, and we aspire to understand it in terms of sensibility, that is, as an expression conveying a systematic association between sense and sensitivity. The central concepts in this book are all terms of sensibility. Such concepts are particularly difficult to use for constructing theories. Understanding them requires descriptions rather than hypotheses. Moral concepts are not typically emotive terms, but they are terms of sensibility. I have delineated the semantic field of the concept of the decent society around terms of sensibility. We should see to it that they also make sense.

Notes

Introduction

1. Karl Popper, *The Open Society and Its Enemies*, vol. 1, *Plato*, 5th ed. (London: Routledge, 1966), pp. 284–285.

2. Jon Elster, "States That Are Essentially By-Products," in Elster, *Sour Grapes* (Cambridge: Cambridge University Press, 1983), pp. 43–101.

1. Humiliation

1. R. Michels, *Political Parties* (New York: Free Press, 1915), p. 13. Michels's work inspired the anarchist argument here, but the argument itself is not his.

2. William Morris, *Editions, Selections, Letters: The Collected Works of William Morris*, intro. Morry Morris, 24 vols. (1910–1915); William Morris, *News from Nowhere*, ed. James Redmond (London: Routledge, Chapman & Hall, 1970).

3. Max Stirner, *Der Einzige und sein Eigentum* (Berlin, 1845), English version, *The Ego and His Own*, trans. Steven T. Byington (London, 1907).

4. David Friedman, *The Machinery of Freedom* (New York: Harper & Row, 1973).

5. Friedrich Nietzsche, *On the Genealogy of Morals*, trans. Walter Kaufmann and R. J. Hollingdale (New York: Vintage Books, 1969), First Essay, Section 10, p. 36.

6. Ibid., p. 39.

2. Rights

1. For example, Thomas E. Hill, "Servility and Self-Respect," *Monist* 57 (1973): 87–104.

2. Joel Feinberg, "The Nature and Value of Rights," *Journal of Value Inquiry* 4 (1970): 243–257. For additional references on this topic, see Meyer J. Michael, "Dignity, Rights and Self-Control," *Ethics* (1984): 520–535.

3. Honor

1. D. Sacks, "How to Distinguish Self-Respect from Self-Esteem," *Philosophy & Public Affairs* (1981): 346–360.

4. Justifying Respect

1. Immanuel Kant, *Groundwork of Metaphysics of Morals*, trans. H. J. Paton, 2nd ed. (New York: Liberal Arts, 1953), esp. p. 77; Kant, *The Doctrine of Virtue*, trans. May J. Gregor (New York: Harper Torchbooks, 1964), esp. p. 434; Lewis W. Beck, *A Commentary on Kant's "Critique of Practical Reason"* (Chicago: University of Chicago Press, 1960), esp. p. 226; Victor J. Seidler, *Kant, Respect, and Injustice* (London: Routledge, Chapman & Hall, 1986).

2. Bernard Williams, "The Idea of Equality," in Joel Feinberg, ed., *Moral Concepts* (London: Oxford University Press, 1969), esp. pp. 159ff.

5. The Skeptical Solution

1. Walt Whitman, "Song of Myself," *Leaves of Grass*, 32.

6. Being Beastly to Humans

1. Nelson Goodman, *The Languages of Art* (Indianapolis: Hackett, 1976).

2. Ludwig Wittgenstein, *Philosophical Investigations*, trans.

G. E. M. Anscombe (Oxford: Basil Blackwell, 1958), pp. 193–219.

3. Stephen Mulhall, *On Being in the World* (London: Routledge, 1990).

4. Moshe Halbertal and Avishai Margalit, *Idolatry* (Cambridge, Mass.: Harvard University Press, 1992).

5. Oliver Sacks, *The Man Who Mistook His Wife for a Hat and Other Clinical Tales* (New York: Harper & Row, 1970).

6. Denis Silk, "Vanishing Trick," in Silk, *Catwalk and Overpass* (New York: Viking, 1990), p. 42.

7. Erwin Goffman, *Stigma* (London: Penguin, 1968).

8. The expression the "Family of Man" comes from the title of a large exhibition of photographs in the fifties, following which there appeared a famous photo book with the same title. In Paris the exhibition was called "The Great Family of Man." Roland Barth, in his book *Mythologies* (trans. Annette Larers, London: Jonathan Cape, 1972, pp. 100–102), noted that the addition of the word "Great" in the French translation of the title turned a neutral concept of the unity of the human species from a "zoological" concept into a sentimental moral notion of a myth that the entire human species lives like one great family. Barth challenged the humanistic trend of assuming a common "nature" underlying all historical and cultural differences, which turns the differences among people into something superficial.

The expression I use here, the "Family of Man," is meant to denote the moral significance of the "zoological" term. I assume that Barth would also deplore my use of the expression as suffering from humanistic sentimentality, if only because I invest it with moral significance. I do not think that my use of the "Family of Man" creates similarities in places where they do not exist, or that it blurs differences in places where they do exist.

9. G. W. F. Hegel, *The Phenomenology of Mind*, trans. J. B. Baillie (New York: Harper & Row, 1967), pp. 229–240.

10. Paul Veyne, "The Roman Empire," in Veyne, ed., *A History of Private Life,* trans. Arthur Goldhammer (Cambridge, Mass.: Harvard University Press, 1987).

11. Ibid., pp. 55ff.

7. The Paradox of Humiliation

1. Jean-Paul Sartre, *Being and Nothingness,* trans. Hazel E. Barnes (London: Methuen, 1969).

8. Rejection

1. Gabrielle Taylor, *Pride, Shame, and Guilt* (Oxford: Oxford University Press, 1985).

2. Avishai Margalit and Joseph Raz, "National Self-Determination," *Journal of Philosophy* 87 (1990): 439–461.

3. Isaiah Berlin, "Two Concepts of Liberty," in Berlin, *Four Essays on Liberty* (London: Oxford University Press, 1969), pp. 156–162.

4. Judith N. Shklar, "Putting Cruelty First," in Shklar, *Ordinary Vices* (Cambridge, Mass.: Harvard University Press, 1984).

9. Citizenship

1. T. H. Marshall, *Class, Citizenship, and Social Development* (New York: Anchor, 1965).

10. Culture

1. Joseph Raz, "Free Expression and Personal Identification," in Raz, *Ethics in the Public Domain* (Oxford: Clarendon, 1994), pp. 131–154; Raz, "Multiculturalism: A Liberal Perspective," ibid., pp. 155–176.

2. Edna Ullmann-Margalit, "On Presumption," *Journal of Philosophy* 3 (1983): 143–163; Ullmann-Margalit, "Some Pre-

sumptions," in Leigh S. Cauman et al., eds., *How Many Questions? Essays in Honor of Sidney Morgenbesser* (Indianapolis: Hackett, 1983).

11. Snobbery

1. See Judith Shklar's insightful account in the chapter "What Is Wrong with Snobbery?" in her book *Ordinary Vices*.

2. Norbert Ellis, *Uber den Prozess der Zivilisation*, 2 vols., 2nd ed. (Frankfurt: Suhrkamp, 1976).

12. Privacy

1. Jean L. Briggs, *Never in Anger: Portrait of an Eskimo Family* (Cambridge, Mass.: Harvard University Press, 1970); Barrington Moore, Jr., *Privacy: Studies in Social and Cultural History* (New York: M. E. Sharpe, 1984), pp. 4–14.

13. Bureaucracy

1. Max Weber, "Bureaucracy," in Guenther Roth and Claus Wittich, eds., *Economy and Society* (New York: Bedminster Press, 1968).

2. Charles Taylor, "The Need for Recognition," in Taylor, *The Ethics of Authenticity* (Cambridge, Mass.: Harvard University Press, 1992); Berlin, "Two Concepts of Liberty."

14. The Welfare Society

1. Maurice Bruce, *The Coming of the Welfare State* (London: B. T. Batsford, 1961); A. William Robson, *Welfare State and Welfare Society: Illusion and Reality* (London: George Allen & Unwin, 1971); Harold L. Wilensky, *The Welfare State and Equality* (Berkeley: University of California Press, 1975); Richard M.

Titmuss, *Essays on the Welfare State* (London: Unwin University Books, 1950).
2. Bruce, *The Coming of the Welfare State*, p. 109.
3. Ibid., p. 51.
4. Nietzsche, *On the Genealogy of Morals*, Preface.
5. Benedict Spinoza, *Ethics*, in Edwin Curley, ed., *The Collected Works of Spinoza* (Princeton: Princeton University Press, 1985).
6. Ludwig von Mises, *Human Action: A Treatise on Economics*, 3rd rev. ed. (Chicago: Henry Regency, 1966), p. 238.
7. Titmuss, *Essays on the Welfare State*.

15. Unemployment

1. Maurice Cranston, *What Are Human Rights?* (London: Bodley Head, 1973), pp. 91–92 (Appendix A).
2. P. Samuelson, "The Normative and Positivistic Inferiority of Marx's Value Paradigm," *Southern Economic Journal* 49 (1982): 11–18.
3. The discussion of exploitation is based mainly on G. A. Cohen, *Karl Marx's Theory of History: A Defence* (Oxford: Oxford University Press, 1978); J. Roemer, *A General Theory of Exploitation and Class* (Cambridge, Mass.: Harvard University Press, 1982); Jon Elster, *Making Sense of Marx* (Cambridge, Mass.: Harvard University Press, 1985), chap. 4.

16. Punishment

1. Michel Foucault, *Discipline and Punish: The Birth of Prison*, trans. Alan Sheridan (London: Allen Lane, 1977).
2. Ibid., chap. 2.

Conclusion

1. John Rawls, *A Theory of Justice* (Cambridge, Mass.: Harvard University Press, 1971).

2. Michael Walzer, *Spheres of Justice: A Defence of Pluralism and Equality* (Oxford: Blackwell, 1983).

3. Albert O. Hirschman, *Exit, Voice, and Loyalty: Responses to Decline in Firms, Organizations, and States* (Cambridge, Mass.: Harvard University Press, 1970).

4. Avishai Margalit, "Ideals and Second-Bests," in Seymour Fox, ed., *Philosophy for Education* (Jerusalem: Van-Leer Foundation, 1983), pp. 77–90.

5. R. Lipsey and K. Lancaster, "The General Theory of Second-Best," *Review of Economic Studies* (1957).

6. Harry G. Frankfurt, "On Bullshit," in Frankfurt, *The Importance of What We Care About* (Cambridge: Cambridge University Press, 1988), pp. 117–134.

Index